# OPERA CLA$

Richard Wagner

# *Der Fliegende Holländer*

## (THE FLYING DUTCHMAN

### OPERA STUDY GUIDE with LIBRETTO

**OPERA STUDY GUIDE with LIBRETTO**

- *Commentary and Analysis*
- *Principal Characters and Story Synopsis/Overview*
- *Story Narrative with Music Highlight Examples*

*with COMPLETE LIBRETTO*

**Edited by Burton D. Fisher**

THIS PAGE INTENTIONALLY LEFT BLANK

Richard Wagner

# *Der Fliegende Holländer*

## (THE FLYING DUTCHMAN)

# OPERA STUDY GUIDE

AND

# LIBRETTO

## OPERA CLASSICS LIBRARY™SERIES

Edited by Burton D. Fisher
Principal lecturer, *Opera Journeys Lecture Series*

*Opera Journeys*™ Publishing　/　Boca Raton, Florida

**WEB SITE: www.operajourneys.com    E MAIL: operaj@bellsouth.net**

# Contents

*Opera Journeys™ Mini Guide Series*

*Opera Classics Library™ Series*

*Opera Journeys™ Libretto Series*

*A History of Opera:*
*Milestones and Metamorphoses*

*Mozart's Da Ponte Operas*

*PUCCINI COMPANION*

*Verdi Companion: 27 Opera Study Guide*

### Over 125 GUIDES & LIBRETTI AVAILABLE: Print or Ebook

•The Abduction from the Seraglio •Adriana Lecouvreur •L'Africaine •Aida
•Andrea Chénier •Anna Bolena •Ariadne auf Naxos •Armida •Attila
•The Ballad of Baby Doe •The Barber of Seville •Duke Bluebeard's Castle
•La Bohème •Boris Godunov •Candide •Capriccio •Carmen
•Cavalleria Rusticana •Cendrillon •La Cenerentola •La Clemenza di Tito
•Le Comte Ory •Così fan tutte •The Crucible •La Damnation de Faust
•The Death of Klinghoffer •Doctor Atomic •Don Carlo •Don Giovanni
•Don Pasquale •La Donna del Lago •The Elixir of Love •Elektra •Ernani
•Eugene Onegin •Exploring Wagner's Ring •Falstaff •La Fanciulla del West
•Faust •La Fille du Régiment •Fidelio •Die Fledermaus •The Flying Dutchman
•Die Frau ohne Schatten •Der Freischütz •Gianni Schicchi •La Gioconda
•Hamlet •Hansel and Gretel •Henry VIII •Iolanta •L'Italiana in Algeri
•Les Huguenots •Iphigénie en Tauride •Julius Caesar •Lakmé •Lohengrin
•Lucia di Lammermoor •Macbeth •Madama Butterfly •The Magic Flute
•The Makropolis Case •Manon •Manon Lescaut •Maria Stuarda
•The Marriage of Figaro •A Masked Ball •Die Meistersinger •The Mikado
•Nabucco •Nixon in China •Norma •Of Mice and Men •Orfeo ed Euridice
•Otello •I Pagliacci •Parsifal •The Pearl Fishers •Pelléas et Mélisande
•Porgy and Bess •Prince Igor •I Puritani •The Queen of Spades
•The Rake's Progress •The Rape of Lucretia •The Rhinegold •Rigoletto
•The Ring of the Nibelung •Roberto Devereaux •Rodalinda •Roméo et Juliette
•La Rondine •Der Rosenkavalier •Rusalka •Salome •Samson and Delilah
•Show Boat •Siegfried •Simon Boccanegra •La Sonnambula •Suor Angelica
•Susannah •Il Tabarro •The Tales of Hoffmann •Tannhäuser •Thaïs •Tosca
•La Traviata •Tristan and Isolde •Il Trittico •Les Troyens •Il Trovatore
•Turandot •The Valkyrie •Werther •West Side Story •Wozzeck

# WWW.OPERAJOURNEYS.COM

## a *Prelude........*

### OPERA CLASSICS LIBRARY's
# *Der Fliegende Holländer*
## STUDY GUIDE AND LIBRETTO

Wagner's *The Flying Dutchman* maintains a special interest in the evolution of modern opera: the opera contains many of the first fruits of Wagner's revolutionary theories — factors that would eventually transform operatic architecture, form and style.

Wagner introduced idealized conceptions of music drama — the *Gesamtkunstwerk*, or the total artwork.

Beginning with the *Dutchman*, Wagner became the great narrator of musical drama: he would seek dramatic truth in the lyric theater by combining the kinetic power of prose with the emotive intensity of music.

*OPERA CLASSICS LIBRARY* explores the greatness of Wagner's *Der Fliegende Holländer*. The *Commentary and Analysis* deals with the opera's genesis, biographical and chronological elements and its premiere and performance history.

The text also contains a *Brief Story Synopsis, Principal Characters,* and a *Story Narrative with Music Highlight Examples,* the latter containing original music transcriptions that are interspersed within the story's dramatic exposition. In addition, the text includes a *Dictionary of Opera and Musical Terms.*

The *Libretto* provides the translation in a side-by-side format (parallel) and includes *Music Highlight Examples.*

The opera art form is the sum of many artistic expressions: theatrical drama, music, scenery, poetry, dance, acting and gesture. In opera, the music composer who is the dramatist; he applies the emotive power of his music and the kinetic intensity of the prose to provide powerful theater, an impact on one's sensibilities that can reach into the very depths of the human soul.

Burton D. Fisher
Editor
OPERA CLASSICS LIBRARY

# *Der Fliegende Holländer*

## (THE FLYING DUTCHMAN)

## Opera in German in three acts

**Music**
**by**
**Richard Wagner**

**Libretto**
**by**
**Richard Wagner**

**After Heinrich Heine's**
***Aus den Memoiren des Herren von Schnabelewopski***
**"The Memoirs of Mr. Schnabelewopski" (1834)**

**Premiere: Dresden, January 1843**

### Commentary and Analysis

During Wagner's first creative period, 1839 — 1850, his opera style was fundamentally subservient to existing operatic traditions and conventions: he faithfully composed in the German Romantic style of Carl Maria von Weber (*Die Freischütz*), Giacomo Meyerbeer's grandiose French style (*Le Prophète, L'Africaine, Robert le Diable, Les Huguenots*), and the Italian bel canto style. The operatic architecture within those genres was primarily concerned with effects, atmosphere, characterization, and actions and climaxes, all presented with formal arias and ensemble numbers, choruses, scenes of pageantry, and in *Tannhäuser*, a ballet.

Wagner's operas from this early period were: *Die Feen* ("The Fairies") based on Carlo Gozzi's *La Donna Serpente* ("The Serpent Woman"), an opera that was never performed during the composer's lifetime but premiered in 1888, five years after his death; *Das Liebesverbot* ("The Ban on Love") (1836), a fiasco based on Shakespeare's *Measure for Measure; Rienzi, Der Letze Der Tribunen* ("Rienzi, Last of the Tribunes") (1842), a resounding success that was based on a Bulwer-Lytton novel; *Der Fliegende Holländer*, ("The Flying Dutchman") (1843); *Tannhäuser* (1845); and *Lohengrin* (1850).

During Wagner's second period, 1850 — 1882, he composed *The Ring of the Nibelung, Tristan und Isolde, Die Meistersinger,* and *Parsifal.* In those later works, Wagner incorporated his revolutionary theories about opera — a new form of lyric theater he called "music drama."

In 1839, at the age of 26, Wagner was an opera conductor at a small, provincial opera company in Riga, Latvia, the country at the time ruled by Russia. In a very short time, he was summarily dismissed, his rambunctious conducting style provoking disfavor, and his heavy debts becoming scandalous — to avoid creditors and debtors' prison, Wagner fled to Paris, the center of the European opera world.

Wagner arrived in Paris with the lofty ambition to become its brightest star, imagining fame and wealth. He appeared with letters of introduction to the "king" of opera, Giacomo Meyerbeer, and his yet uncompleted score for *Rienzi.*

During Wagner's three years in Paris — from 1839 to 1842 — he experienced agonizing hardships: he lived in penury and misery, and survived mostly by editing, writing, and performing musical "slave work" by transcribing operas for Jacques Halévy. The leading lights of French opera were Meyerbeer and Halévy, but Wagner was unsuccessful in securing their help and influence in having *Rienzi* produced at the Paris Opéra. He turned to despair: he became lonely and alienated, frustrated by his failures, and deeply bitter. His dreams were shattered, and his Paris years became a hopeless adventure, the non-French speaking Wagner considered himself an outsider.

Nevertheless, during his Parisian years, he completed both *Rienzi* and *The Flying Dutchman*, an incredible accomplishment since both operas possess extremely diverse stories and musical styles. *Rienzi* was a melodrama composed in the Italian bel canto style: it portrays the tribulations of its protagonist in conflict with power politics. *Dutchman* was composed in a unified, musically integrated style: it recounts the legend of a sailor doomed to travel the seas until he is redeemed by a faithful woman's love.

In 1842, the omnipotent Meyerbeer, changed the young composer's fortunes and used his influence to persuade the Dresden opera to produce *Rienzi. Rienzi* became an outstanding success, actually, the most successful opera during Wagner's lifetime; although it is frequently revived in the contemporary repertory, it has become overshadowed by Wagner's later works.

Nevertheless, *Rienzi* catapulted Wagner to operatic stardom, prompting the Royal Saxon Court Theater in Dresden to appoint him Kapellmeister — the year was 1843, and Wagner was twenty-nine-years-old. That same year, *The Flying Dutchman* was mounted at Dresden to a rather mediocre reception; it was followed by *Tannhäuser* (1845), and *Lohengrin*, introduced by Franz Liszt at Weimar in 1850.

During the second half of the nineteenth century, Wagner revolutionized opera with his conceptions of music drama: he created a seamless continuity between opera's internal architectural elements by virtually eliminating the formal structures of recitative and aria (or set piece); the result became a seamless continuity of music and text in the evolving drama. Through leading motives, or leitmotifs, the orchestra exposed the thoughts and ideas of the characters, but the orchestra was now transformed from accompanist into a symphonic unit; it became an integral protagonist of the drama that provided "endliche melodie," or an endless chain of music.

Wagner's *Tristan and Isolde* is vast in its concept and design, bold in its execution, revolutionary in its operatic structure, and exacting in its demands on singers and the orchestra. In this opera, Wagner's music-drama esthetics were first materialized: the extensive use of leitmotifs, the integration of the orchestra into the drama, and the dramatic unity of all its artistic elements.

The leitmotif of the entire music drama is the exaltation of love: as Wagner commented, "a monument to this loveliest of all dreams." In this opera, Wagner spiritualized love: an ideal beyond experienced emotions or the material world that is consummated metaphysically, or as a transcendent experience.

Musically, *Tristan and Isolde* represents a milestone — if not a revolution — in the history of music: its music emancipated dissonance from tonality and set the stage for future harmonic adventurism; the music score of *Tristan and Isolde* has been deemed the beginning of modern music, Wagner's harmonic innovations continuing into modern times. The score is dominated by discords, an innovation that broke all the existing rules of tonality: for hundreds of years before *Tristan and Isolde*, the essence of music was tonality; all music was composed in keys, chords could be identified with keys, or identified as transitional chords between keys.

The "Tristan Chord" — f, b, d sharp, g sharp, appearing initially in the second full measure of the Prelude and associated with Grief or Sorrow — is perhaps the most famous chord in the history of music, its essence challenging conventional analysis. The Tristan Chord is a discord; it partially resolves and it is partially suspended, creating a sense of both resolution and dissonance. As the music progresses new discords are created: the result is that the ear becomes partially satisfied by the resolution, but dissatisfied by the suspension; a lack of resolution that creates a sense of tension as the listener consciously and unconsciously craves for resolution. Wagner built the harmonics of the entire opera on discord and lack of resolution, except the final chord, its resolution suggesting a finality: the culmination of insatiable yearning.

*Tristan and Isolde*'s premiere was scheduled for Vienna in 1859. However, the premiere was abandoned after some fifty-seven rehearsals, the musicians finding Wagner's score virtually impossible to learn and play, and the singers finding it unsingable. Its music was so revolutionary that Wagner was considered seriously insane, a musical anarchist and iconoclast intent on destroying Western music traditions. But the opera did have its premiere six years later and Wagner's ingenious harmonic innovations began to overtake the music world. After Wagner, many composers began to abandon tonality; it began a transformation in music's harmonic structure, such as the introduction of the atonal, 12-tone, or serial music, an avant-garde technique that virtually considered conventional melody, rhythm and traditional harmony evil elements of the musical language.

Wagner's early operas, from *Die Feen* (1834) ("The Fairies"), after Carlo Gozzi's *La Donna Serpente* ("The Serpent Woman"), through *Lohengrin* (1850), derived from Wolfram von Eschenbach's *Parzifal*, reflect strong musical and aesthetic influences from the German Romantic as well as the Italian bel canto schools: those operas contain many parallels to the mysticism and spiritualism of Weber's *Oberon* (1826) and Marschner's *Der Vampyr (*1828), as well as the Italian bel canto masters, Rossini and Belllini.

Wagner vehemently opposed the abuses of the Italian bel canto school: their hackneyed librettos, obsession with spectacle, and showcases for singers: to Wagner, much of opera that preceded him was "causes without effects." Wagner shared Berlioz's description of the genre: "Music of the Italians is a sensual pleasure and nothing more. For this noble expression of the mind, they (the Italians) have hardly more respect than for the art of cooking. They want a score that, like a plate of macaroni, can be assimilated immediately without having to think about it, or even pay attention to it."

Nevertheless, Wagner's operas prior to 1850, particularly *Tannhäuser* and *Lohengrin*, possess intense lyricism and represent perhaps the pinnacle of the bel canto school: Wagner, at times the principal antagonist of Italian bel canto, ironically became its foremost and finest practitioner. But Wagner was seeking an antidote for the existing conventions of recitative, set-pieces, or numbers, that he considered elements that impeded the flow of the drama. In his next compositional period, beginning in the 1850s, he would develop theories of music drama that would completely transform opera traditions.

Wagner's challenge was to let drama run an unbroken course without restraining the action with purely musical forms. As such, he envisioned a complete fusion of drama and music, in which the drama would be conceived in terms of music, and the music would freely work according to its own inner laws, a balance in which the drama assisted but did not constrain the music. The words had to share equally with the music in realizing the drama, their inflections sounding ideally in alliterative clusters with the vocal line springing directly out of the natural rise and fall of the words. As such, the voices were to give the impression of heightened speech, and the ultimate opera would become a "sung drama." However, where words failed, the orchestra would convey the drama through recurring musical themes, what Wagner called "motifs of memory," that were later termed leitmotifs.

In 1849, Wagner's participation in the Dresden political uprisings caused him to become exiled from Germany. He found safe haven in Zurich, where he began to pen his theories about opera: *Die Kunst und die Revolution* ("Art and Revolution"); *Die Kunst der Zukunft* ("The Artwork of the Future"); and *Oper und Drama* ("Opera and Drama"). Essentially, these were theories that envisioned the opera art form as a "Gesamtkunstwerk," a complete work of art that incorporated all artistic and creative elements: acting and gesture, poetry, music, and scenery; opera was idealistically a total artistic unity that was the sum of its various parts. As such, Wagner conceived opera as music drama: the full integration of text, music, and other artistic elements that contribute to realizing the drama.

Wagner's first attempt to put his theories and conceptions into practice began in 1848: he began his monumental trilogy, *Der Ring des Nibelungen* ("The Ring of the Nibelung.") In 1864, Wagner was rescued from financial disaster by Ludwig II, an impassioned admirer who had just acceded to the throne of Bavaria. With the King's support, Wagner produced *Tristan and Isolde* (1865), *Die Meistersinger* (1868), premiered the two *Ring* operas *Das Rheingold* (1869) and *Die Walküre* (1870), opened the Bayreuth Festspielhaus in 1876 with the full production of *The Ring of the Nibelung,* and completed his final opera, *Parsifal* (1882).

*Mein Leben* ("My Life") was Wagner's autobiography, a self-serving chronology and interpretation of his life and works that he began in the 1860s after achieving world-wide fame and recognition. Many of Wagner's recollections require a judicious separation of fiction from fact, particularly since after Wagner's death, his widow Cosima supervised what many consider a prejudicial editing of the work.

In *Mein Leben,* Wagner vividly described his inspiration for composing *Der Fliegende Holländer.* In the summer of 1839, Wagner was a conductor in Riga, Latvia. Accompanied by his wife Minna, then in the first stages of pregnancy, they boarded the *Thetis,* a small schooner that crossed the North Sea from Pillau on the Baltic coast of East Prussia — to London, and then to Paris; they decided to sail to Paris via London and chance what would become a perilous three week sea voyage — at the time, the cheapest way to reach Paris.

The seldom gentle North Sea was experiencing brutal weather conditions: the *Thetis* was nearly wrecked three times by a violent storm, and in one instance, it was compelled to seek safety in a Norwegian harbor. According to Wagner's autobiography, those experiences inspired the opera, *Der Fliegende Holländer.*

He later recalled the sounds of sailors echoing from the granite walls of the Norwegian harbor of Sandviken, an inspiration for Daland's call to the Dutchman in Act I, *"Werda?",* and, the Norwegian Sailors' Chorus, "Steuermann! Lass die Wacht!" Wagner commented that those musical inspirations were "like an omen of good cheer that shaped itself presently into the theme of the seamen's song in my *The Flying Dutchman."* Wagner would portray the experiences of the terrifying voyage through deeds of music: a ferocious and merciless sea, and an unceasingly restless ocean with raging storms that dominate the *Dutchman* score.

Wagner was a prolific reader of German Romantic literature; he was well familiar with Heinrich Heine's haunting story of *The Flying Dutchman: Aus den Memoiren des Herren von Schnabelewopski* ("The Memoirs of Herr Von Schnabelewopski"), a retelling of the nautical legend about the doomed seaman, from *Der Salon* (1834).

Heine (1797 — 1856) was a preeminent German Romantic lyric poet and writer during the early decades of the nineteenth century. Wagner was not only inspired to *The Flying Dutchman* from Heine's works, but his later *Tannhäuser* owes much of its provenance to Heine's poem, *Der Tannhäuser* (1836): Heine's lively evocations of the young Siegfried in *Deutschland ist noch ein kleines Kind* (1840) would certainly influence elements of *Der Ring des Nibelungen.*

Heine was a romantic poet whose writings were set to music by composers such as Franz Schubert and Robert Schumann. He was also a gifted satirist and political writer whose fierce attacks on repression, injustices and prejudices esstablished his reputation as a highly controversial figure. Heine was a German who made Paris his permanent home. While he witnessed the establishment of limited democracy in France, he became increasingly critical of the political and social movements that were affecting nineteenth-century Germany. Eventually, his popularity enraged and angered the German government; he sparked controversy that prompted the government to ban all of his works, a clear refutation that convinced him that he was no longer welcome in his homeland.

Heine was a quintessential lyric poet: his brief poems were not narrative, but expressed personal thoughts and feelings. Lyric poetry evolved during medieval times and was originally intended to be sung to musical accompaniment. But during the nineteenth-century Romantic era transformation, the poems tended to be melodic through their inherent rhythmic, song-like patterns: musical accompaniment was abandoned and word-play was intended to evoke powerful and energetic sensibilities.

Throughout his life, Heine considered himself an outsider. He was a Jew in a nation plagued by anti-Semitism, and consequently developed an inescapable sense of alienation, isolation and loneliness. He considered himself "a Jew among Germans, a German among Frenchman, and a Helene among Jews, a rebel among the bourgeois, and a conservative among revolutionaries."

Heine's *Aus den Memoiren des Herren Schnabelewopski*, the story that became Wagner's underlying basis for *The Flying Dutchman* is virtually autobiographical — Heine himself was the alienated, isolated and lonely Dutchman. Similarly, Richard Wagner had suffered agonizing frustration and defeat during his Paris years, and wholeheartedly identified with the isolation that affected the hero of Heine's story.

Consciously and unconsciously, Wagner's muse was inspired by his personal identification with his protagonists: all of the characters in Wagner operas represent the composer himself. At the time of *Dutchman,* Wagner was exceedingly unhappy, bankrupt, unemployed and a failed composer. The melancholy Dutchman symbolized his own wretched condition — a man persecuted, uprooted and unfulfilled. The Dutchman was seeking redemption, and likewise, Richard Wagner.

In the spring of 1841, Wagner moved to Medufon, a small village a short distance from Paris where he wrote the original prose scenario for the *Dutchman;* it was presumably completed during a seven weeks period.

He submitted the first sketch of the libretto to Léon Pillet, director of the Paris Opéra. Wagner's financial condition was so dismal that he regretfully sold Pillet the libretto for 500 francs. Nevertheless, he did reserve the German rights. Under the contract, Wagner did not receive the commission to compose the opera: that was granted to Pierre-Louis Dietsch. The Dietsch opera was entitled *Le Vaisseau Fantôme* ("The Phantom Ship"). Librettists Paul Foucher and Bénédict-Henry Révoil based their story not only on Wagner's scenario, but also on other sources: Captain Marryat's novel *The Phantom Ship;* Sir Walter Scott's *The Pirate,* with elements of the legend written by Heinrich Heine, James Fenimore Cooper and Wilhelm Hauff. Nevertheless, Wagner continued to compose his *Dutchman* to his own libretto.

Wagner's *Der Fliegende Holländer* was produced in Dresden after the phenomenal success of *Rienzi*. In November 1842, Dietsch's *Le Vaisseau Fantôme* premiered at the Opéra in Paris almost simultaneously — it was a signal failure. As Wagner began rehearsals for the *Dutchman*, the Paris premiere of Dietsch's opera was undoubtedly one reason for inserting eleventh-hour changes in the score. Wagner emphatically distanced himself from Dietsch's work in order to avoid a collision. Therefore, he transformed the story's venue from Heine's Scottish coast to the Norwegian coast, and replaced the characters of Donald and George with Daland and Erik respectively.

Wagner himself conducted the première, which featured Wilhelmine Schröder-Devrient, the renowned soprano, as the heroine Senta. The *Dutchman* aroused antipathy from its premiere audience who concluded that although the opera possessed a somber beauty, its thematic orientation was overly psychological. Wagner's *Dutchman* was canceled after its fourth performance.

It was revived twenty-two years later at a time when Wagner's operas had been achieving world-wide acclaim. Even then, it was considered a failure, but Ludwig Spohr, the renowned composer and violinist, was almost alone in acclaiming the excellence of the work, and in proclaiming Wagner the most gifted contemporary composer for the lyric theater.

Wagner originally conceived the *Dutchman* in a single act, claiming that a one-act opera enabled him to better focus on the opera' intrinsic dramatic essentials. The Paris Opéra had rejected Wagner's proposal for a one-act opera. As such, he developed the scenario in three distinct acts, the form in which it was given in Dresden at its premiere, and subsequently published. Nevertheless, in 1901, Cosima Wagner introduced it in its one-act version at Bayreuth, and ever since, there have been many one-act productions.

After its Dresden premiere, Wagner made many revisions to the score: among the many, alterations in the orchestration, and a remodeling of the coda of the Overture. Like the Paris version of *Tannhäuser*, many of his revisions reflected his preoccupation and advancements that he had effected and developed in *Tristan und Isolde*.

*Der Fliegende Holländer* contains many innovations of traditions and conventions with respect existing operatic structure and architecture.

In particular, Wagner began to find his inspiration in mythical or legendary subjects, thematic elements that would dominate his entire oeuvre. Wagner's underlying concept was that myth and legend reflected basic humanity; as such, they offered the composer powerful elements for artistic and dramatic expression.

Wagner envisioned the legend as a means of comprehending purely human aspects of a people, an age or a nation: therefore, it provides a form of easily intelligible insight. He envisioned the legend as a great source of human truth, easily comprehensible and easily explanable within the course of the inner motives of the action and that of the soul.

Wagner considered himself a musical dramatist, and he could no longer intelligently express dramatic truth within existing operatic traditional and conventions. subjects in a conglomeration of operatic arias and set-pieces. Indeed, he was accused of iconoclasm by eliminating arias in the *Dutchman*, set pieces that had heretofore been considered the soul of opera. In *Rienzi*, Wagner succeeded in using a combination of existing operatic conventions and traditions: arias, set-pieces and ensembles. But he found those techniques impracticable for the *Dutchman* story: existing conventions that would prevent him from conveying the full emotional impact inherent in the text.

Wagner found is music growing out of the nature of the scenes — traditional forms of operatic music would interrupted the organic development that he had envisioned in his scores. Yes, Wagner was a deliberate reformer, but the destruction of the aria, duet, and other operatic forms followed consistently from the nature of his subjects.

Wagner stressed the importance of using representative themes, what have been called "leading motives" or leitmotifs. Wagner had reached the conclusion that in opera, the music must become the handmaid of poetry; therefore, the musical formulae must be sacrificed. He believed that once the best musical investiture of a particular emotion had been discovered, he had to associate its reappearance with the same musical expression. The result became leitmotifs, or "leading motives" which were designed to represent a particular person, mood or thought within the overall dramatic scope of the work. In *Dutchman*, Wagner's use of leitmotifs was in its infancy: in *Tristan und Isolde* and in particular, *Der Ring des Nibelungen*, they had reached full development.

In effect, Wagner found that the old operatic structures were incompatible with the systematic use of leitmotifs; consequently, beginning with *Dutchman*, for the most part, he abandoned set-pieces, trios, or quartets.

In Senta's *Ballad*, Wagner found the seeds of his future musical leitmotif system. The *Ballad* comprises two themes that represent the fundamental essence of the drama: first, the Dutchman's motive, in which the accursed wanderer yearns for inner peace; and second, Senta's redemption motive, which expresses the sacrificial love of the eternal woman. These two themes develop and mold the *Ballad*, their recall significant in achieving ideal thematic expression and dramatic truth.

Wagner fashioned these revolutionary transformations on the organic union of poetry, painting, music and action. Beginning with *Dutchman*, these elements would become so fully integrated, that no one aspect could be regarded as more important than the other: as such, opera became a total art form in which the whole became equal to the sum of its parts, what Wagner termed the *Gesamtkunstwerk*.

R omantic period artists felt alienated from the rest of society, the isolation attributed to society's inability to completely understand or appreciate the acute sensibilities inherent in the creative spirits. Some artists deliberately sought to separate themselves from society in order to engage in quiet contemplation and introspection; others totally rejected society's attitudes and values.

Heine expressed the artist's inner sensibilities: "The artist is the child in the popular fable, every one of whose tears was a pearl. Ah! The world, that cruel stepmother, beats the poor child the harder to make him shed more pearls."

In Paris, Wagner's personal emotions and sense of alienation and loneliness were synonymous with those of the Dutchman: the Dutchman was a weary mariner, yearning for land and love; Wagner was a weary artist, homesick and longing for his fatherland. The churning anguish and intense suffering within Wagner's soul were synonymous with those of his *Dutchman*. In the end, both were in desperate need of redemption.

Johann Wolfgang von Goethe endowed the German Romanticist movement with the ideal of the eternal female: the "ewige weibliche" or "femme eterne" was the sacrificing woman who inspired man toward infinitely greater achievements. German Romanticists ennobled the "woman of the future" as the redeemer of man through sacrifice and unbounded love. In *Dutchman*, the embodiment of that exalted woman became the character of

Senta, the opera's heroine. Wagner's ideal women would reappear in his later works: Elizabeth in _Tannhäuser_, Brünnhilde in the _Ring_ operas and Isolde in _Tristan und Isolde_.

The _Dutchman_ represented the beginning of Wagner's evolutionary continuum: the suffering, alienated outsider redeemed by the eternally faithful woman.

Senta's _Ballad_ contains the thematic nucleus of the eternal, redeeming woman. It is in the _Ballad_ that the Dutchman's blasphemy is revealed: as such, the _Ballad_ integrates the identifying themes of the Dutchman himself with Senta's theme of redemption. Nevertheless, Senta's _Ballad_ is structurally typical of the early nineteenth-century tradition of narrative song, and Wagner was well familiar with one of its German Romantic role-models: in Marschner's _Der Vampyr_, Emmy's song possesses many similarities to the three turbulent stanzas of Senta's _Ballad_.

In Senta's final refrain, she is overcome by a sudden inspiration and explodes into ecstatic rapture as she expresses her determination to be the instrument of the Dutchman's salvation. Wagner surpassed Heine by creatively elevating Senta's character to that of nobility: her fidelity and love are the engines that provide the dramatic thrust of the opera — the embodiment of the "ewige weibliche" so treasured by German Romantics.

Wagner musically differentiates the opera's other characters. In the Dutchman's opening Monologue, "Die Frist ist um" the harmonies project a self-absorbed world, while the harmonies in the music of Daland, Erik and the Norwegian sailors represent the exterior world. Wagner ingeniously created the Dutchman's character as other-worldly, a character that is far from conventional.

In Erik's _Dream Narration_, Wagner provides a precursor to tose that appear in his more mature works: narrations are integral aspects of _Tannhäuser, Lohengrin,_ and his later music dramas. Erik recounts his dream about Senta's father bringing home a stranger who resembles the seafarer of the painting. Senta becomes engrossed in a hypnotic trance, that brings life to her compassion through her trance-like rapture.

The drama possesses chiaroscuro, extreme musical and visual contrasts. The Norwegians have a robust naturalness, strongly contrasted by the supernatural ghostliness of everything related to the Dutchman and his ship, its silence and phantomlike sailing and docking.

In the third act, the musical contrast is more delineated: Wagner becomes a choreographer as sailors break out in song and dance, their dancing accented by a heavy foot-stomping downbeat. In contrast, the girls interplay with the Dutch sailors is grim and deathly.

In the final scene, the Norwegian sailors taunt the eerie crew of _The Flying Dutchman:_ "Have you no letter, no message to leave, we can bring our great-grandfathers here to receive?" Wagner was adopting Heine's mention of an English ship bound for Amsterdam that was hailed on the seas by a Dutch vessel: its crew gave a sack of mail to the Englishmen asking that its contents be delivered to the proper parties in Amsterdam. Upon reaching their destination, the English crew was chilled to find that many of the addressees had been dead for over 100 years.

Wagner claimed that with the _Dutchman,_ he began his career as a true musical poet. Musically, the opera certainly marks a great step beyond the Meyerbeerian, bel canto style of _Rienzi:_ an assured development of his musical and dramatic ideas. It is in _Dutchman_ that Wagner first uses an appreciable number of leitmotifs which the orchestra interweaves with ingenious virtuosity. The opera's singleness of conception and mood, and almost total elimination of set-pieces anticipates a synthesis of text and music — the seeds and ideological beginnings of "through-composition" that would be integral to Wagner's future music dramas.

*The Flying Dutchman* maintains a special interest for all Wagnerians: it exhibits the first fruits of Wagner's revolutionary theories, factors that contributed to a complete transformation of modern operatic architecture, form and style. Although the opera fails to reach the complete individuality and overwhelming power of Wagner's later works, many aficionados of early Wagner wish that he had composed at least one more opera in the old, romantic tradition of *The Flying Dutchman*.

*Lohengrin*, composed between 1846 and 1848, was Wagner's last opera before he reinvented himself and introduced his idealized conception of music dramas — the *Gesamtkunstwerk*. Wagner would cut the cord that had tied him to the past and totally abandon old paths and strike-out in new directions with his new esthetics: Wagner would no longer compose operas, but rather, he would become the creator of music dramas.

In essence, the *Dutchman* represented a turning point in the development of musical drama. With the *Dutchman*, Wagner launched himself as the great narrator of musical drama. He sought dramatic truth in the lyric theater by combining the kinetic power of prose with the emotive intensity of music.

### Principal Characters in Der Fliegende Holländer

Van der Decken, captain of the ship, *The Flying Dutchman*  Baritone
Daland, a Norwegian sea-captain                              Bass
Senta, Daland's daughter                                     Soprano
Erik, a huntsman                                             Tenor
Steersman                                                    Tenor
Mary, Senta's nurse                                          Mezzo-soprano

Norwegian sailors, the Dutchman's crew,
young Maidens from the Norwegian village

**TIME:**   18th century
**PLACE:** Coast of Norway

### Brief Story Synopsis

The legend about *The Flying Dutchman* — as told by Heine and embellished by Wagner — relates the story of Van der Decken, a Dutch sea captain, who impiously invoked the devil to assist him in rounding the stormy Cape of Good Hope: he was punished for his blasphemy and doomed to sail the seas eternally. However, once every seven years, he was allowed to come ashore to seek salvation: if he found a woman who vowed eternal love and faith, "true unto death," he would be released from his punishment.

The opera story begins simultaneously with the start of one of the Dutchman's seven-year pardons. A storm has driven his ship to shelter: at the same time, a Norwegian ship, captained by Daland, finds safety in the same harbor.

Daland meets the Dutch captain and proceeds to raves about Senta, his daughter. The Dutchman immediately expresses his desire to marry her. Daland has become impressed by the Dutchman's wealth and easily agrees.

Although Senta has never met the Dutchman, his portrait hangs on the wall of Daland's house. She is well familiar with the legend of his curse, and vows to rescue him and become his redemptive woman: "true unto death." Daland introduces the Dutchman to Senta: they immediately fall in love and agree to wed.

Erik, a huntsman and suitor of Senta, berates her, condemning her desire to marry the Dutchman as an act of betrayal. The Dutchman overhears them argue, misunderstands Senta's entreaties to Erik, and believes that she has already betrayed him.

He releases Senta from her vows and sails from the harbor. Senta pursues the Dutchman by mounting a cliff and casting herself into the deadly seas, her sacrificial death serving to redeem the Dutchman.

As *The Flying Dutchman* vanishes in the mist, the united lovers are seen ecstatically embraced as they rise toward the heavens.

### Story Narrative with Music Highlight Examples

#### Overture:

The Overture to *Der Fliegende Holländer* provides the imagery of a furious, raging and tempestuous storm at sea: amidst the tension, the brass resounds with the thunderous theme associated with the Vanderdecken, the Holländer, a sailor condemned to travel the seas until he is redeemed by a woman's faithful love.

#### The Flying Dutchman's Theme:

The second theme represents Senta's redeeming love for the Dutch seaman.

#### Senta's Theme: Redemption

#### Act I: the rocky coast of Norway

A raging storm along the coast has driven a Norwegian ship to seek cover. The ship drops anchor in the safety of a cover. The sailors unfurl the sails, their shouts of "Hojohe! Halojo!" echo from the cliffs. Daland, the ship's captain, goes ashore, climbs upon a rocky cliff and survey the coast. He concludes that the storm has led them into the bay of Sandwicke, forty miles from their home port.

The Norwegian sailors go below to rest. Alone on deck, the Steersman remains on watch at the helm, barely generating enough energy to stay awake. He arouses himself by singing a seaman's song: "Mit Gewitter und Sturm aus fernem Meer, Mein Mädel, bin dir nah'!" ("Through bad weather and storms from the distant seas, my maiden, I will be close") — the song expressing hope for a favorable south-wind that will return him home to his love. After losing his struggle with fatigue, he falls asleep.

#### Mein Mädel, wenn nicht Südwind wär

The sky darkens, and the storm begins to rage again. Another ship enters the cove and drops anchor alongside the Norwegian ship. The ship is _The Flying Dutchman_, a ghostly ship with blood-red sails and black hull. The sound of its anchor crashing into the water awakens the Steersman. He becomes baffled after looking about: is satisfied that no harm has been done to the ship, and returns to a few more verses of his pining seaman's song, and then falls off to sleep again.

Silently, the spectral crew of _The Flying Dutchman_ unfurls its black sails. Afterwards, Vanderdecken, the ship's captain appears, a man with a dark beard and a pallid face. As he goes ashore, he comments that seven years have passed, and that he has reached land again: "Die Frist ist um, und abermals verstrichen" ("The time is up, and to Eternity's tomb I am consigned.")

The Holländer explains his despair and desolation: he swore that he could defy the gods and sail the Cape of Good Hope. He was cursed for his vanity: he was condemned to sail the seas and permitted to land but once every seven years — his curse removed if he is redeemed by the love of a faithful woman.

He pleads earnestly for deliverance from his accursed doom, but he fears that there is no hope for salvation —death would be a welcome, merciful pardon: "Wie oft in Meeres tiefsten Schlund" ("How often I have sought death and eternal sleep in the ocean's depths.") He remains forlorn, and meditates silently.

### _Wie oft in Meeres tiefsten Schlund_

Daland observes the strange ship and awakens the Steersman, reproaching him for sleeping while on duty. He calls out to the ship, but there is no response, only the echoes from his shouts of "Werda?" ("Ahoy.") Daland notices that the ship's captain is ashore, and proceeds to approach him.

Van der Decken introduces himself simply as a "Holländer" and then proceeds to provide Daland with an account of his endless voyaging: "Durch Sturm und bösen Wind verschlagen" ("Storm and raging winds wind have kept me from shore.")

### _Durch Sturm und bösen Wind_

The Holländer explains that he has neither wife nor family. Daland informs him of his daughter, Senta. Suddenly, the Holländer ovewhelms Daland with an offer of him treasure from his cargo in exchange for his hospitality as well as his daughter's hand in marriage.

Daland is incredulous by the Holländer's generous offer: greed, as well as the stranger's interest in his daughter prompts him to agree: "Wie? Hört' ich recht? Meine Tochter sein Weib?" ("My child shall be his, why should I delay?")

Daland assures the Holländer that his daughter shall be a faithful wife. The Holländer becomes impatient and asks to see her at once, envisioning that she will bring peace to his tormented soul.

*Wenn aus der Qualen Schreckge walten,*

The storm subsides, and a south-wind enables both ships to weigh anchor and sail toward Daland's house.

### Act II: a large room in Daland's house

Mary, Senta's nurse and housekeeper, together with maidens, are busy at their spinning wheels. Their spinning is symbolic: a prayer for favorable winds to speed their lovers' to them.

Senta sits in a chair, absorbed in dreamy contemplation. She gazes fixedly at a portrait of a pale man with dark beard wearing Spanish attire, the portrait possessing an uncanny resemblance to Van der Decken, the captain of *The Flying Dutchman.*

The Spinning Song chorus "Summ' und brumm'" ("Hum and buzz") with its repetitive melodies and rhythms evoke the humdrum labor in their spinning.

### Spinning Chorus

Senta iremains absorbed in viewing the portrait. She sighs, wondering why she has such insight and compassion for the fate of this wretched man? Mary reproaches her for being idle, but the other women excuse her, commenting that she need not spin because her lover is not a sailor, but rather, a hot-tempered hunter of game.

Senta responds angrily to the women's foolish jesting. They respond to her chiding by singing loudly and rapidly spinning in order to drown her out with a deafening noise.

To stop them, Senta asks Mary to sing the *Ballad* about *The Flying Dutchman,* but Mary refuses. Senta decides to sing the *Ballad* herself.

In anticipation, the maidens group around Senta's chair while Mary continues spinning. Senta begins the *Ballad:* "Johohoe! Johohohoe!" She describes The Flying the Dutchman, the Holländer's ghostly ship, with its blood-red sails and black masts, and its blasphemous captain, condemned to roam the seas until he finds a woman faithful and true.

She exudes intgense compassion as she prays that he will find that woman and be rescued from his eternal torment.

### *Trafft ihr das Schiff im Meere an?*

As Senta recounts that the Holländer comes ashore every seven years to seek a faithful wife, she becomes possessed: she rises from her chair, as if consumed by a sudden inspiration. She becomes ecstatic and declares that she will become the Holländer's faithful bride, the instrument of redemption and salvation that will rescue him from his unfortunate fate. Senta addresses her vision to the portrait: "Ich sei's die dich durch ihre Treu' er löse!" ("I will be the woman who by her love will save you!")

### *Theme of Redemption*

Senta's outcry horrifies Mary and the maidens, some suggesting that they believe that she has become mad.

Erik, a huntsman in love with Senta, suddenly enters to announce that he has seen the sails from Daland's ship. The news that the men are returning prompts the women to leave and prepare to welcome their men-folk.

Erik restrains Senta from leaving, and immediately pours out his love for her. He pleads with her to accept his humble lot and marry him before her father decides to find her a wealthier husband: "Mein Herz voll Treue bis zum Sterben" ("A loving heart alone, I bring thee.")

### *Mein Herz voll Treue bis zum Sterben.*

Senta shuns Erik, heedless to his ardent pleas for her love. Erik relates a dream in which her father brought a stranger home who resembled the seaman in the portrait. He asked for her hand in marriage and she agreed, afterwards fleeing with him on his ghostly ship.

As Senta listens, she becomes overcome by her imagination: she erupts into ecstatic rapture and proclaims that she is determined to share the Holländer's fate.

In fear and despair, Erik rushes away.

### *Auf hohem Felsen lag'ich träumend*

Alone, Senta is absorbed in thought, her eyes remaining fixed on the portrait. Softly, but with profound emotion, she recalls the "redemption" refrain from her *Ballad:* "Ach! Möchtest du, bleicher Seemann, sie finden! Betet zum Himmel, dass bald ein Weib Treue ihm" (" Ah! You mighty, pallid seaman, find her! Pray to Heaven that soon your wish will be granted!")

Senta's last words are unfinished when suddenly the door opens, and Daland and the captain of The Flying Dutchman stand before her at the threshold. Senta turns her gaze from the portrait to the Holländer, and then utters an uncontrollable cry of astonishment — she then turns mute and spellbound, her eyes continuing to stare fixedly on the Holländer.

The Holländer moves toward Senta, likewise, his eyes remain firmly fixed upon her. Daland stands at the door, bewildered that his daughter has not greeted him, and proceeds to reproach her for not welcoming him with a kiss and an embrace. Senta seizes her father's hand and draws him closer to her; she welcomes him and immediately inquires of the stranger's identity.

Daland introduces the Holländer in a breezy and lighthearted manner: "Mögst du, mein Kind" ("Will you my child, kindly welcome a stranger!") He explains that the man has wandered from afar and earned treasures amid dangers in foreign lands; however, he was banished from his homeland, and would richly pay for a home. He asks Senta if it would displease her if he should stay with them?

Daland inquires if Senta would consent to marry the stranger; he tempts her by displaying some of the Holländer's jewels. But only the Holländer interests her as her eyes remain transfixed on him: likewise, the Holländer is absorbed in contemplation of Senta.

Daland becomes perplexed by their mysterious silence and decides to leave them alone. As he departs, he seeks the Holländer's confirmation that his daughter is indeed as fair and charming as he had promised.

Senta and the Dutchman remain motionless, absorbed in mutual contemplation of one another. Then he declares that his dreams have transformed into reality, and informs Senta that she is the woman whom he has yearned for, the angel who can bring peace to his tormented soul.

### Wohl hub auch ich voll Sehnsucht meine Blicke

Senta and the Holländer become absorbed by their individual inner thoughts: Senta wonders whether she is dreaming, while the Holländer wonders if it is indeed true that his dream of salvation has become a reality.

Senta vows to the Holländer that he will be redeemed from his curse through her love — that she will be his love angel who will bring him joy.

Senta pledges eternal faith and fidelity to the Holländer— until death.

Both become rapturous as they celebrate their new-found love.

### Was ist's das mächtig in mir lebet

Daland appears, curious as to whether the feast of homecoming can be combined with a betrothal. Senta reaffirms her vows to the Dutchman, and all three join together and express their rapturous joy.

### Act III: the bay near Daland's home

It is a clear night. In the background, partly visible and moored near one another, are the ships of Vanderdecken and Daland; high cliffs above the sea rise some distance away.

The Norwegian ship is illuminated, the sailors indulging in merriment on its deck. In contrast, *The Flying Dutchman* possesses an unnatural darkness and deathly stillness.

Young girls emerge from their houses bearing food and drink, and the Norwegian sailors excitedly invite them to join with them.

### Steuerman! Lass die Wacht!

The girls are confounded by the Dutch ship: it is dark, unlit and appears to have no crew. The Norwegian sailors jest, suggesting that The Flying Dutchman sailors have no need for refreshments since their crew is asleep; or perhaps they are all dead. The sailors call out to

*The Flying Dutchman's* crew, inviting them to join in the merriment. There is no response, only an eerie silence, prompting the girls to tremble in fear and retreat from the ship.

A dark bluish flame flares up like a beacon on the *The Flying Dutchman,* causing its crew — hitherto invisible — to become aroused; they talk about their captain, now on land, who is seeking a faithful bride.

The sea begins to whirl around The Flying Dutchman as frightful winds whistle, and the ship is tossed about by the raging waves; elsewhere, the air and winds remain calm.

The Norwegian sailors become bewildered by the appearance of *The Flying Dutchman's* crew; they believe that they are ghosts, and in fear and terror, they make the sign of the cross.

The Flying Dutchman crew observes their motions and burst into shrill laughter. Suddenly, the air and sea calm, and in the eerie darkness a deathly stillness overcomes their ship.

Senta emerges from her house, trembling and in agitation: Erik follows her, likewise irritated and disquieted. Erik has become possessed by depair and demands to know why she betrayed him and decided to marry the Dutchman. He implores Senta, reminding her that she had vowed her eternal love to him.

### *Willst jenes Tag's di nicht dich mehr entsinnen*

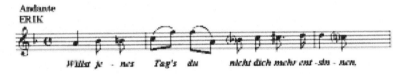

Senta denies him, explaining that she is compelled to the Holländer by a higher power: she disavows Erik and urges him to forget her. Unnoticed, the Holländer has been overhearing them argue. In particular, he hears Erik's last words in which he reminds Senta that she promised to be true to him: "Versich'rung, die Versich'rung deiner treu'?" ("Did you not promise to be true?")

He misunderstands them and erupts into uncontrollable agitation as he cries out: "Verloren! Ach! Verloren! Ewig verlor'nes Heil!" ("Lost! All is forever lost.") Erik steps back in astonishment as the Holländer approaches Senta, shouting to her: "Senta, leb'wohl!: ("Senta, farewell!")

Senta turns towards the departing Holländer angily shouts out in despair: "In See für ew'ge Zeiten!" ("To Sea! For eternity!") He reproaches Senta for betraying her promise, heedless to her pleas for him to remain.

The Holländer signals to his crew with his pipe, thier order to weigh anchor and set sail immediately: a farewell forever to land and hope. With great agitation, he condemns Senta as unfaithful — that her promise to him was frivolous, a mockery.

Senta assures him that her promises will be kept, and that she will be true to him.

Erik looks on, exacerbated and convinced that Senta has become possessed by the Devil.

The Holländer vindicates Senta by assuring her that she will be free from eternal damnation because she did not make her vows before God; nevertheless, she has shattered his hopes for eternal peace, and he continues to be doomed to roam the seas for eternity.

Senta protests, and again assures theHolländer that she has been true — that a love vowed unto death shall remove his curse.

The Holländer rushes to board his ship. The sailors hoist their crimson sails and put to sea. A storm suddenly begins to rage.

Erik has become concerned about Senta's sanity and calls for help. Daland, Mary and maidens rush from the house, and Norwegian sailors leave their ship. All attempt to restrain Senta from pursuing the Holländer.

Senta struggles to free herself. She ascends a cliff overhanging the sea an looks toward the departing Flying Dutchman. Suddenly, she bursts into an ecstatic outcry and proclaims her unbounded fidelity to the departing Holländer: ("Your angel has been commanded. I am faithful to you even unto death.")

Afterwards, Senta casts herself into the sea.

Suddenly, the sea rises. *The Flying Dutchman* is wrecked and sinks into a violently spinning whirlpool.

In the glow of the sunset, the transfigured images of Senta and the Holländer are seen, eternally embraced as they rise from the sea toward the heavens.

# *Libretto*

## Act I — Scene 1

*After being driven by a violent storm, a Norwegian ship anchors in a calm cove at Sandwicke, forty miles from its home port.*
*Sailors busily unfurl the sails as Daland, the Norwegian captain, goes ashore; he has scaled the rocky cliffs to survey the seacoast.*

**Die Masterosen:**
Hojohe! Hallojo!
Hojohe! Hallojo! Ho! He!
Ho! He! Ja! Ho! Hallojo!
Ho! Johe! Hallohe! Hallohe!

**Sailors:** *(at work)*
Hojohe! Hallojo!
Hojohe! Hallojo! Ho! He!
Ho! He! Ja! Ho! Hallojo!
Ho! Johe! Hallohe! Hallohe!

**Daland:**
Kein Zweifel! Sieben Meilen fort
trieb uns der Sturm vom sichren Port.
So nah' dem Ziel nach langer Fahrt,
war mir der Streich noch aufgespart!

**Daland:** *(disembarking the ship)*
No doubt! The storm has blown us seven
miles from the safety of our port.
So near our harbor after a long voyage
and now this bad luck!

**Steuermann:**
Ho! Kapitän!

**Steersman:** *(on board, shouting)*
Ho! Captain!

**Daland:**
Am Bord bei euch, wie steht's?

**Daland:**
How's everything on board?

**Steersman:**
Gut, Kapitän! Wir haben sichren Grund!

**Steersman:**
All's well, Captain. We're safe here.

**Daland:**
Sandwike ist's! Genau kenn' ich die Bucht.
Verwünscht! Schon sah am Ufer ich mein
Haus, Senta, mein Kind, glaub' ich schon zu
umarmen: da bläst es aus dem Teufelsloch
heraus! Wer baut auf Wind, baut auf Satans
Erbarmen!

Was hilft's? Geduld! Der Sturn lässt nach;
wenn er so tobte, währt's nicht lang.

He, Bursche! Lange war't ihr wach;
zur Ruhe denn! Mir ist nicht bang!

Nun, Steuermann, die Wache nimmst du
wohl für mich? Gefahr ist nicht, doch gut
ist's, wenn du wachst.

**Daland:'**
Sandwike it is. I know the bay well.
Confound it! I saw my home.
Senta, my child, I seemed to be embracing
her, but
then this devilish gale blew up!
If one trusts the wind, trust Satan's mercy!
*(going aboard)*
Any good news Patience! The storm is
abating; that rage cannot last.

Ho, lads! Your watch was long.
Rest now! There's nothing to fear here

Now, helmsman, take the watch for me?
There's no danger but you had better stay
awake.

**Steersmann:**
Seid ausser Sorg'! Schlaft ruhig, Kapitän!

**Steersman:**
Rest easy! Sleep in peace. Captain!

*Daland leaves to enter his cabin; the Steersman remains alone on deck.*
*The storm has abated, although the waves remain rough out at sea.*
*The Steersman makes another round, then sits down near the helm.*
*He yawns, then rouses himself, as if he had inadvertently fallen asleep.*

**Steuermann:**             **Steersman:**

Mit Gewitter und Sturm aus fernem Meer,
mein Mädel, bin dir nah!
Über turmhohe Flut vom Süden her,
mein Mädel, ich bin da!
Mein Mädel, wenn nich Südwind wär',
ich nimmer wohl käm' zu dir:
Ach, lieber Südwind, blas noch mehr!
Mein Mädel verlangt nach mir!
Hohojo! Hallohoho!
Jollohohoho! Hohoje!
Hallohoho! ho ho ho ho ho ho!

My maiden, I am near you! Whether in gale
or storm in from far-off seas.
After overcoming towering waves from the
south, my maiden, I am here!
My maiden, were there no southwind,
I could never have sailed here!
Ah, dear south-wind, blow stronger!
My maiden longs for me!
Hohojo! Hallohoho!
Jollohohoho! Hohoje!
Hallohoho! ho ho ho ho ho ho!

*A wave violently wave shakes the ship. The Steersman starts up, then looks around, having*
*satisfied that no harm has been done. He sits down again near the helm and sings,*
*occasionally yawning, and than gradually falling asleep.*

**Steuermann:**
Von des Südens Gestad', aus weitem Land
ich hab an dich gedacht;
durch Gewitter und Meer vom
Mohrenstrand
hab dir was mitgebracht.
Mein Mädel, preis den Südwind hoch,
ich bring dir ein gülden Band;
Ach, lieber Südwind, blase doch!
Mein Mädel hätt' gern den Tand.
Hoho! Je! holla ho!

**Steersman:**
I thought of you, while on southern shores,
in far-off lands!
Through storms and sea, from Moroccan
coast
I have brought you something:
my maiden, praise the south-wind,
I bring you a golden ring.
Ah, dear south-wind, blow stronger!
My maiden would like the trinket.
Hoho! Je! holla ho!

*The Steersman struggles with his fatigue and finally falls asleep. The storm begins to rage*
*again: it grows darker. In the distance, the ship of the Flying Dutchman appears,*
*with blood-red sails and black masts. She rapidly nears the shore,*
*and weighs anchor opposite the Norwegian ship. With a fearful crash she drops anchor.*
*The Steersman is suddenly awakened from his sleep, glances hastily, and begins his song.*

**Steuermann:**
Mein Mädel, wenn nicht Südwind wär'. .

**Steersman:**
My maiden, were there no south-wind...

### Act I— Scene 2
*The Steeresman falls asleep once more.*
*With utter silence, the spectral crew of the Dutchman infurls the sails.*
*The Dutchman goes ashore, wearing black Spanish cloathing.* ?   22:35

**Holländer:**
Die Frist ist um, und abermals verstrichen
sind sieben Jahr': voll Überdruss wirft mich
das Meer ans Land. Ha, Stolzer Ozean!
In kurzer Frist sollst du mich wieder tragen!
Dein Trotz ist beugsam, doch ewig meine
Qual.
Das Heil, das auf dem Land ich suche, nie
werd ich es finden! Euch, des Weltmeers
Fluten, bleib' ich getreu, bis eure letzte
Welle sich bricht und euer letztes Nass versiegt!

**Holländer:**
The time is up and seven more years
have passed. The weary sea casts me up
on land. Ha! proud ocean!
Soon you shall bear me again!
Your spite is fitful, but my torment is
eternal!
I shall never find the grace I seek on land!
To you, ocean-tides,
I shall be true, until your last wave
breaks, and you are drained dry.

Allegro molto
DUTCHMAN

*Wie oft im Meer — es tiefsten Schlund stürz'ich voll Sehnsucht mich hinab.*

Wie oft in Meeres tiefsten Schund
stürzt' ich voll Sehnsucht mich hinab,
doch ach! den Tod, ich fand ihn nicht!
Da, wo der Schiffe furchtbar Grab,
trieb mein Schiff ich zum Klippengrund;
doch ach! mein Grab, es schloss sich nicht.

How often have I longingly hurled myself
into the sea's deepest jaws
yet death, ah, I found it not!
There, in the awful tomb of ships,
I drove mine on to the rocks,
but alas, no tomb closed over me!

Verhöhnend droht' ich dem Piraten,
in wildem Kampfe hofft' ich Tod.
Hier — rief ich — zeige deine Taten,
von Schätzen voll sind Schiff und Boot!
Doch ach! des Meer's barbar'scher Sohn
schlägt bang das Kreuz und flïgt davon!
Nirgends ein Grab! Niemals der Tod!
Dies der Verdammis Schreckgebot.

Mockingly, I defied the pirate,
I hoped for death in fierce combat.
Here — I cried — show your prowess.
M ship is filled with treasure.
Alas, the sea's barbarous son
crossed himself in terror and fled!
Nowhere a grave! Never death!
This is damnation's dread command!

Dich frage ich, gepreisner Engel Gottes,
der meines Heils Bedingung mir gewann;
war ich Unsel'ger Spielwerk deines Spottes,
als die Erlösung du mir zeigtest an?
Vergebne Hoffnung! Furchtbar eitler Wahn!
Un ew'ge Treu auf Erden ist's getan!

I ask you, blessed angel of God,
who won the terms of my salvation,
was I the sorry plaything of your scorn,
when you showed me the path to
redemption? Vain hope! Terrible, futile folly!
There is no eternal fidelity on earth!

Nur eine Hoffnung soll mir bleiben,
nur eine unerschüttert stehn:
solang der Erde Keim' auch treiben,
so muss sie doch zugrunde gehn!

Tag des Gerichtes! Jüngster Tag!
Wann brichst du an in meine Nacht?
Wann dröhnt er, der Vernichtungschlag,
mit dem die Welt zusammenkracht?
Wann alle Toten auferstehn,
dann werde ich in Nichts vergehn.
Ihr Welten, endet euren Lauf!
Ew'ge Vernichtung, nimm mich auf!

**Chor der Mannschaft des Holläders:**
Ew'ge Vernichtung, nimm uns auf!

Only one hope is left to me,
only one that is undestroyed:
while Earth's seeds long may thrive,
yet it too must end one day!

Day of Judgment! Day of Doom!
When will you dawn and end my night?
When will the crack of doom resound,
rending the earth asunder?
When all the dead rise up,
then shall I fade into the void.
Worlds, end your course!
Eternal destruction, take me!

**The Holländer's Crew:** *(from the hold)*
Eternal destruction, take us!

## Act I — Scene 3

*Daland comes on deck, he checks the wind direction, and then notices the foreign ship.*

**Daland:**
He! Holla! Steuermann!

**Daland:** *(looking for the steersman)*
Hey there! Steersman!

**Steuermann:**
's ist nichts! 's ist nichts!
""Ach, lieber Südwind, blas noch mehr,
mein Mädel..."

**Steersman:** *(sleepily)*
It's nothing! It's nothing!
"Ah, dear south-wind, blow stronger,
my maiden..."

**Daland:**
Du siehst nichts? Gelt, du wachest brav,
mein Bursch!
Dort liegt ein Schiff. Wie lange schliefst du
schon?

**Daland:** *(awakening the steersman)*
You see nothing? Fine watch you keep,
don't you, lad?
There lies a ship. How long have you been
asleep?

**Steuermann:**
Zum Teufel auch! Verzeiht mir, Kapitän!

**Steersman:** *(starting up quickly)*
Devil take it! Pardon me, Captain!

*He takes a megaphone and calls across to the mysterious ship alongside.*

Wer da?

Who are you?

*An echo is heard, and then a long pause.*

Wer da?

Who are you?

**Daland:**
Es scheint, sie sind gerad so faul als wir.

**Daland:**
They seem just as lazy as we are.

**Steuermann:**
Gebt Anwort! Schiff und Flagge?

**Steersman:**
Answer! Your ship and flag?

**Daland:**
Lass ab! Mich dünkt, ich seh' den Kapitän!

He! Holla! Seemann! Nenne dich! Wes
Landes?

**Daland:** *(sees the Dutchman on shore)*
Wait! I think I see the Captain.
*(calling the Holländer)*
Ahoy there! Sailor! Your name! Where are
you from?

**Holländer:**
Weit komm ich her; verwehrt bei Sturm und
Wetter ihr mir den Ankerplatz?

**Holländer:**
I come from afar: would you deny me
anchorage in this storm?

**Daland:**
Behüt es Gott!
Gastfreundschaft kennt der Seemann!

Wer bist du?

**Daland:**
God forbid!
A sailor is always hospitable!
*(going ashore)*
Who are you?

**Holländer:**
Holländer.

**Holländer:**
A Holländer.

**Daland:**
Gott zum Gruss! So trieb auch doch
der Sturm an diesen nackten Felsenstrand?
Mi ging's nicht besser: wenig Meilen nur
von hier ist meine Heimat; fast erreicht,
musst' ich aufs neu mich von ihr wenden.
Sag,
woher kommst du? Hast Schaden du genommen?

**Daland:**
God's greeting! So the storm also drove you
to this barren rocky beach?
I was no luckier: my home is only a few
miles from here: I was almost there
when I had to turn about.
Say,
where are you from? Are you damaged?

**Holländer:**
Mein Schiff ist fest, es leidet keinen Schaden.

**Holländer:**
My ship is strong, she is undamaged.

Durch Sturm und bösen Wind verschlagen,
irr auf den Wassern ich umher, wie lange?
weiss ich kaum zu sagen, schon zähl ich
nicht die Jahre mehr.
Unmöglich dünkt mich's, dass ich nenne
die Länder alle, die ich fand: das eine nur,
nach dem ich brenne, ich find es nicht, mein
Heimatland! Vergönne mir auf kurze Frist
dein Haus und deine Freundschaft soll dich
nicht gereun.

I roam the seas, driven on by storms and ill
winds, how long, I can hardly tell;
I no longer count the years.
It is impossible to name
all the lands that I have found:
the only one I long for
I cannot find: my homeland!
Grant me a short stay in your home,
and you won't regret your friendship.

Mit Schätzen aller Gegenden und Zonen ist
reich mein Schiff beladen: willst du handeln,
so sollst du sicher deines Vorteils sein.

**Daland:**
Wie wunderbar! Soll deinem Wort ich
glauben? Ein Unstern, scheint's, hat dich bis
jetzt verfolgt. Um dir zu frommen, biet ich,
was ich kann, doch darf ich fragen, was dein
Schiff enthält?

**Holländer:**
Die seltensten der Schätze sollst du sehn,
kostbare Perlen, edelstes Gestein.
Blick hin, und überzeuge dich vom Werte
des Preises, den ich für ein gastlich' Dach
dir biete!

**Daland:**
Wie? Ist's möglich? Diese Schätze!
Wer ist so reich, den Preis dafür zu bieten?

**Holländer:**
Den Pries? Soeben hab ich ihn genannt;
dies für das Obdach einer einz'gen Nacht!
Doch, was du siehst, ist nur der kleinste
Teil von dem, was meines Schiffes Raum
verschliesst.
Was frommt der Schatz? Ich habe weder
Weib noch Kind, und meine Heimat find ich
nie! All meinen Reichtum biet ich dir, wenn
bei den Deinen du mir neue Heimat gibst.

**Daland:**
Was muss ich hören!

**Holländer:**
Hast du eine Tochter?

**Daland:**
Fürwahr, ein treues Kind.

**Holländer:**
Sie sei mein Weib!

**Daland:**
Wie? Hör ich recht?
Meine Tochter sein Weib?

My ship is richly laden with treasures from
every land and area: if you'll agree,
you'll profit by it.

**Daland:**
How wonderful! Can I believe you?
Ill-luck seems to have dogged you.
To help you
I'll offer what I can:
but — may I ask what your ship holds?

**Holländer:** *(his crew brings a chest ashore)*
You shall see the rarest treasures,
costly pearls, precious stones.
*(The chest is opened)*
Look and satisfy yourself of the value
of what I offer for a friendly roof.

**Daland:** *(amazed by the chest's contents)*
What? Is it possible? This treasure!
Who's rich enough to offer a price for it?

**Holländer:**
The price? I have just named it:
all this for one night's shelter!
Yet what you see
is but the smallest part
of what is stowed in my ship's hold.
What use is treasure? I have neither wife
nor child, and my home I shall never find!
All my riches I offer you, if
you give me a new home with your family.

**Daland:**
What do I hear?

**Holländer:**
Have you a daughter?

**Daland:**
Indeed I have, a good child.

**Holländer:**
Let her be my wife!

**Daland:** *(joyfully astonished)*
What? Did I hear correctly?
My daughter his wife?

Er selbst spricht aus den Gedanken!
Fast fürcht ich, wenn unentschlossen ich
bleib, er müsst' im Vorsatze wanken.
Wüsst' ich, ob ich wach' oder träume?
Kann ein Eidam willkommener sein?
Ein Tor, wenn das Glück ich versäume!
Voll Entzücken schlage ich ein!

**Holländer:**
Ach, ohne Weib, ohne Kind bin ich,
nichts fesselt mich an die Erde;
rastlos verfolgte das Schicksal mich,
die Qual nur war mir Gefährte.
Nie werd ich die Heimat erreichen,
zu was frommt mir der Güter Gewinn?
Lässt du zu dem Bund dich erweichen,
o! so nimm meine Schätze dahin!

**Daland:**
Wohl, Fremdling, hab ich eine schöne
Tochter, mit treuer Kindeslieb' ergeben mir;
sie ist mein Stolz, das höchste meiner
Güter, mein Trost im Unglück, meine
Freund' im Glück.

**Holländer:**
Dem Vater stets bewahr' sie ihre Liebe!
Ihm treu, wird sie auch treu dem Gatten
sein.

**Daland:**
Du gibst Juwelen, unschätzbare Perlen,
das höchste Kleinod doch, ein treues Weib...

**Holländer:**
Du gibst es mir?

**Daland:**
Ich gebe dir mein Wort.
Mich rührt dein Los; freigebig, wie du bist,
zeigst Edelmut und hohen Sinn du mir:
den Eidam wünscht ich so, und wär dein
Gut
auch nicht so reich, wählt' ich doch keinen
andren!

**Holländer:**
Hab Dank! Werd ich die Tochter heut noch
sehn?

It is his own suggestion!
I almost fear that if I hesitate
he may change his mind.
I don't know if I am awake or dreaming.
Can there be a more welcome son-in-law?
I'd be a fool to miss this chance!
I'm delighted with my luck!

**Holländer:**
Ah, no wife, no child have I,
nothing chains me to this Earth!
A pitiless fate pursues me,
torment was my only companion.
I shall never reach my homeland,
wealth has no value for me?
Just consent to our union,
then take my treasure!

**Daland:**
Yes, stranger, I have a lovely daughter,
devoted to me with the true love of a child:
she is my pride, my greatest blessing,
my comfort in misfortune, my joy in
success.

**Holländer:**
May she always love her father:
as true as she is it him, she'll be as true to
her husband.

**Daland:**
You give jewels, priceless pearls,
but the peerless gem, is a true wife...

**Holländer:**
Are you giving it all to me?

**Daland:**
I give you my word.
I am moved by your grim fate;
generous as you are
you show a noble heart and mind:
I would like that of my son-in-law;
and were you not so rich, I'd still choose no
other.

**Holländer:**
My thanks! Shall I see your daughter
today?

**Daland:**
Der nächste günst'ge Wind bringt uns nach
Haus; du sollst sie sehn, und wenn sie dir
gefällt...

**Daland:**
The first fair wind will take us home,
you shall see her,
and if you like her...

**Holländer:**
So ist sie mein...
(Wird sie mein Engel sein?)

**Holländer:**
She shall be mine...
(Will she be my angel?)

Wenn aus der Qualen Schreckgewalten
die Sehnsucht nach dem Heil mich treibt,
ist mir's erlaubt, mich festzuhalten
an einer Hoffnung, die mir bleibt?
Darf ich in jenem Wahn noch schmachten,
dass sich ein Engel mir erweicht?

When from my terrible anguish
my longing for grace drives me on,
dare I cling
to the one hope left to me?
dare I cherish the idle fancy
that an angel may pity me?

Der Qualen, die mein Haupt umnachten,
ersehntes Ziel hätt' ich erreicht?
Ach! Ohne Hoffnung, wie ich bin,
geb ich mich doch der Hoffnung hin!

Of the torments that bemuse my brain,
have I at last reached the end?
Ah, without hope, I am what I am,
but now, I still surrender to hope!

**Daland:**
Gepreisen seid, gepreisen seid des Sturmes
Gewalten, die ihr an diesen Strand mich
triebt!
Fürwahr, bloss hab ich festzuhalten, was
sich so schön von selbst mir gibt. Die ihn an
diese Küste brachten, ihr Winde, sellt
gesegnet sein!

**Daland:**
Praised be the violent storm
which drove me to this shore!
Truly, I have only to grasp
what he so generously gives me.
You winds,
who brought him to this coast,
I bless you!

Ha, womach alle Väter trachten,
ein reicher Eidam, er ist mein.
Ja! dem Mann mit Gut und hohem Sinn
geb froh ich Haus und Tochter hin!

Ha, what all fathers seek,
a rich son-in-law — is to be mine!
Yes, to a man so rich and noble,
I gladly give my home and daughter.

**Steuermann:**
Südwind! Südwind!

**Steersman:**
South-wind, south-wind!

**Die Masterosen:**
Halloho!

**Sailors:** *(waving their caps)*
Halloho!

**Steuermann:**
Ach, lieber Südwind, blas noch mehr!

**Die Masterosen:**
Hohohe! Halloho!
Hallo ho ho ho ho!

**Daland:**
Du siehst, das Glück ist günstig dir;
der Wind ist gut, die See in Ruh.
Sogleich die Anker lichten wir
und segeln schnell der Heimat zu.

**Holländer:**
Darf ich dich bitten, so segelst du voran:
der Wind ist frisch, doch meine Mannschaft
müd; ich gönn ihr kurze Ruh und folge dann.

**Die Masterosen:**
Ho! Ho! Hallohe!
Hallohe! Hallohohe!

**Steuermann:**
Hallohe! Hallohe!

**Daland:**
Doch, unser Wind?

**Holländer:**
Er bläst noch lang aus Süd.
Mein Schiff ist schnell, es holt dich sicher
ein.

**Daland:**
Du glaubst? Wohlan, es möge denn so sein!
Leb wohl, mögst heute du mein Kind noch
sehn!

**Holländer:**
Gewiss!

**Daland:**
Heil! Wie die Segel schon sich bläh'n!
Hallo! Hallo!

Frisch, Jungen, greifet an!

---

**Steersman:**
Ah, dear south-wind, blow stronger!

**Sailors:**
Hohohe! Halloho!
Hallo ho ho ho ho!

**Daland:**
You see, fortune favors you.
The wind's set fair, the sea is calm.
We'll weigh anchor now
and speedily sail for home.

**Holländer:**
Can I ask you to sail on ahead?
The wind is fresh but my crew are weary.
I'll give a short rest and follow behind.

**Sailors:**
Ho! Ho! Hallohe!
Hallohe! Hallohohe!

**Steersman:**
Hallohe! Hallohe!

**Daland:**
But our wind?

**Holländer:**
It'll blow from the south a long time!
My ship is fast, we'll overtake you for
sure.

**Daland:**
You think so? Maybe.
Farewell! You may still see my daughter
today.

**Holländer:**
Surely!

**Daland:** *(boarding his ship)*
Ha! How the sails swell already!
Hallo! Hallo!
*(he whistles the signal to depart)*
Come on, boys, set to!

**Die Masterosen:**

Mit Gewitter und Sturm aus fernem Meer,
mein Mädel, bin dir nah! Hurrah!
Über turmhohe Flut vom Süden her,
mein Mädel, ich bin da! Hurrah!
Mein Mädel, wenn nicht Südwind wär,
ich nimmer wohl käm zu dir;
Ach, lieber Südwind, blas noch mehr!
Mein Mädel verlangt nach mir.

Hohoho! Johoho!
Hohohohoho!

**Sailors:** *(exultantly, as they sail away)*

In gales and storm from far-off seas,
my maiden, I am near you! Hurrah!
Over towering waves from the south,
my maiden, I am here! Hurrah!
My maiden, were there no south-wind,
I could never come to you.
Ah, dear south-wind, blow stronger!
My maiden longs for me!

Hohoho! Johoho!
Hohohohoho!

**END of ACT I**

### Act II — Scene 1

*A large room in Daland's house; Mary and the girls are seated, many of them spinning.*
*On the walls are pictures related to the sea: ships, maps, et al.*
*On the back wall, a portrait of a man with pale face and dark beard, wearing a black cloak.*
*Senta sits in a chair, lost in contemplation of the portrait on the wall.*

**Die Mädchen:**                         **The Maidens:**

| | |
|---|---|
| Summ und brumm, du gutes Rädchen, | Hum and buzz, good wheel, |
| munter, munter, dreh dich um! | gaily, gaily turn! |
| Spinne, spinne tausend Fädchen, | Spin, spin a thousand threads, |
| gutes Rädchen, summ und brumm! | good wheel, hum and buzz! |
| Mein Schatz ist auf dem Meere draus, | My love is out at sea, |
| er denkt nach Haus | he thinks of home |
| ans fromme Kind; | and his true maiden; |
| mein gutes Rädchen, braus und saus! | my good wheel, hum and sing! |

| | |
|---|---|
| Ach, gäbst du Wind, | Ah, if you drove the wind, |
| er käm geschwind. | he'd soon be here. |
| Spinnt! Spinnt! | Spin! Spin! Spin! |
| Fleissig, Mädchen! | Set to, girls! |
| Brumm! Summ! | Buzz! Hum! |
| Gutes Rädchen! | Good wheel! |
| Tralaralalalala! | Tralaralalalala! |

**Mary:**                              **Mary:**
Ei, fleissig, fleissig, wie sie spinnen!   Aha! Work away! How busily they spin!
Will jede sich den Schatz gewinnen.      Each wants to win a sweetheart!

**Die Mädchen:**                         **The Maidens:**
Frau Mary, still! Denn wohl ihr wisst,   Mistress Mary, hush! You know quite well
das Lied noch nicht zu Ende ist!         the song is not yet finished.

**Mary:**                              **Mary:**
So singt! Dem Rädchen lässt's nicht Ruh.   Then sing! It keeps the wheel working.
                                        *(to Senta)*
Du aber, Senta, schweigst dazu?          But you, Senta, not a word?

| | |
|---|---|
| **Die Mädchen:** | **The Maidens:** |
| Summ und brumm, du gutes Rädchen, | Hum and buzz, good wheel, |
| munter, munter dreh dich um! | gaily, gaily turn! |
| Spinne, spinne tausend Fädchen, | Spin, spin a thousand threads, |
| gutes Rädchen, summ und brumm! | good wheel, hum and buzz! |
| Mein Schatz da draussen auf dem Meer, | My love out there at sea, |
| im Süden er | in the South |
| viel Gold gewinnt; | has won much gold; |
| ach, gutes Rädchen, saus noch mehr! | ah, good wheel, turn faster! |

| | |
|---|---|
| Er gibt's dem Kind, | He'll give it to his girl |
| wenn's fleissig spinnt! | if she spins well. |
| Spinnt! Spinnt! | Spin! Spin! |
| Fleissig, Mädchen! | Work away, girls! |
| Brumm! Summ! | Buzz! Hum! |
| Gutes Rädchen! | Good wheel! |
| Tralaralalalala! | Tralaralalalala! |

| | |
|---|---|
| **Mary:** | **Mary:** *(to Senta)* |
| Du böses Kind! Wenn du nicht spinnst, | You naughty girl, if you don't spin, |
| vom Schatz du kein Geschenk gewinnst. | you'll get no gift from your sweetheart. |

| | |
|---|---|
| **Die Mädchen:** | **The Maidens:** |
| Sie hat's nicht not, dass sie sich eilt; | She has no need to hurry; |
| ihr Schatz nicht auf dem Meere weilt: | her sweetheart's not at sea. |
| bringt er nicht Gold, bringt er doch Wild, | He brings no gold, but game, |
| man weiss ja, was ein Jäger gilt! | we know well what a hunter's worth. |

*They laugh. Senta, without changing her position, softly hums a theme from ballad.*

| | |
|---|---|
| **Mary:** | **Mary:** *(to Senta)* |
| Da seht ihr! Immer vor dem Bild! | Look! Always sitting in front of that picture! |
| Willst du dein ganzes junges Leben | Do you want to dream away your whole |
| verträumen vor dem Konterfei? | young life in front of that portrait? |

| | |
|---|---|
| **Senta:** | **Senta:** |
| Was hast du Kunde mir gegeben, | Why did you tell me? |
| was mir erzählet, wer er sei... | Why did you tell me the story about him? |
| der arme Mann! | The poor man! |

| | |
|---|---|
| **Mary:** | **Mary:** |
| Gott sei mit dir! | God be with you! |

| | |
|---|---|
| **Die Mädchen:** | **The Maidens:** |
| Ei, ei! Ei, ei! Was hören wir! | Aha! What do we hear! |
| Sie seufzet um den bleichen Mann! | She sighs for the pale man! |

**Mary:**
Den Kopf verliert sie noch darum!

**Die Mädchen:**
Da sieht man, was ein Bild doch kann!

**Mary:**
Nichts hilft es, wenn ich täglich brumm!
Komm! Senta! Wend dich doch herum!

**Die Mädchen:**
Sie hört euch nicht! Sie ist verliebt!
Ei, ei! Wenn's nur nicht Händel gibt!
Denn Erik hat gar heisses Blut,
dass er nur keinen Schaden tut!
Sagt nichts! Er schiesst sonst wutentbrannt
den Nebenbuhler von der Wand!

**Senta:**
O schweigt mit eurem tollen Lachen!
Wollt ihr mich ernstlich böse machen?

**Die Mädchen:**

*The Maidens interrupt Senta with comic fervor: they spin loudly,
so as to drown out Senta's intent to scold them.*

Summ und brumm, Du gutes Rädchen,
munter, munter dreh dich um!
Spinne, spinne tausend Fädchen!
Gutes Rädchen, summ und brumm!

**Senta:**
O, macht dem dummen Lied ein Ende!
Es brummt und summt nur vor dem Ohr.
Wollt ihr, dass ich mich zu euch wende,
so sucht was besseres hervor!

**Die Mädchen:**
Gut! Singe du!

**Senta:**
Hört, was ich rate;
Frau Mary singt uns die Ballade.

**Mary:**
Bewahre Gott! das fehlte mir!
Den fliegenden Holläender lasst in Ruh!

---

**Mary:**
She's lost her head over him.

**The Maidens:**
You see what a picture can do!

**Mary:**
It's no use though I grumble daily!
Come, Senta! turn around!

**The Maidens:**
She can't hear you — she's in love!
Oh! Oh! let's hope there'll be no quarrel,
for Erik is very hot-blooded
may he do no violence!
Say nothing or, mad with rage,
he'll shoot his rival off the wall!

**Senta:** *(angrily)*
Oh, stop your silly laughing!
Do you want to really make me angry?

**The Maidens:**

Hum and buzz, good wheel,
gaily, gaily turn!
Spin, spin a thousand threads,
good wheel, hum and buzz!

**Senta:** *(jumping up angrily)*
Oh, stop that stupid song,
it hums and buzzes in my ears!
If you want me with you,
think of something better!

**The Maidens:**
Very well! You sing!

**Senta:**
Hear what I propose:
Let Mistress Mary sing us the ballad.

**Mary:**
God forbid! I could not!
Leave the Flying Dutchman in peace!

**Senta:**
Wie oft doch hört' ich sie von dir!

**Senta:**
Yet I have often heard it from you!

**Mary:**
Bewahre Gott, das fehlte mir!

**Mary:**
God forbid! I could not!

**Senta:**
Ich sing sie selbst! Hört, Mädchen, zu!
Lasst mich's euch recht zum Herzen führen:
des Ärmsten Los — es muss euch rühren!

**Senta:**
I'll sing it myself! Listen, girls!
Let me appeal to your hearts,
the poor man's fate will surely move you!

**Die Mädchen:**
Uns ist es recht!

**The Maidens:**
All right, let's hear it.

**Senta:**
Merkt auf die Wort'!

**Senta:**
Mark well the words.

**Die Mädchen:**
Dem Spinnrad Ruh!

**The Maidens:**
Stop the spinning-wheels!

**Mary:**
Ich spinne fort!

**Mary:** *(crossly)*
I'll spin on!

*The Maidens put their spinning-wheels aside,*
*and group around Senta as she begins singing a Ballad.*
*Mary, however, remains sitting by the hearth and continues her spinning.*

**Senta:**
Johohoe! Johohohoe!
Hohohoe! Johoe!

**Senta:**
Johohoe! Johohohoe!
Hohohoe! Johoe!

Traft ihr das Schiff im Meere an,
blutrot die Segel, schwarz der Mast?
Auf hohem Bord der bleiche Mann,
des Schiffes Herr, wacht ohne Rast.
Hui! Wie saust der Wind! Johohe!
Hui! Wie pfeift's im Tau! Johohe!
Hui! Wie ein Pfeil fliegt er hin,
ohne Ziel, ohne Rast, ohne Ruh!
Doch kann dem bleichen Manne Erlösung
einstens noch werden, fänd er ein Weib, das
bis in den Tod getreu ihm auf Erden!

Have you met the ship at sea
with blood-red sails and black mast?
On the high deck, the pale man,
the master of the ship, keeps endless watch.
Hui! How the wind howls! Yohohey!
Hui! How it whistles in the rigging,
Yohohey! Hui! Like an arrow he flies,
without aim, without rest, without peace!
But redemption may one day come to the
pale man, if he but find a woman on earth
true unto death.

Ach! wann wirst du, bleicher Seemann, sie
finden? Betet zum Himmel, dass bald
ein Weib Treue ihm halt'!

Oh, when will you find her, wan mariner?
Pray to Heaven that soon a woman
will stay true to him!

***Towards the end of the stanza Senta turns to the picture, and stares at it with intensity.***
***The Maidens have been listening attentively; Mary has stopped spinning.***

Bei bösem Wind und Sturmeswut
umsegeln wollt' er einst ein Kap;
er flucht' und schwur mit tollem Mut:
"in Ewigkeit lass' ich nicht ab!"
Hui! Und Satan hört's! Johohe!
Hui! Nahm ihm beim Wort! Johohe!

In bitter gale and raging storm,
he once tried to round a cape;
he cursed, in mad fury, and swore:
"Never will I give up!"
Hui! And Satan heard it! Yohohey!
Hui! Took him at his word! Yohohey!

Hui! Und verdammt zieht er nun
durch das Meer ohne Rast, ohne Ruh!
Doch, dass der arme Mann noch Erlösung
fände auf Erden,
zeigt' Gottes Engel an, wie sein Heil ihm
einst könnte werden:

Hui! And, damned, he now roams
the sea without rest or peace!
But the poor man may still find salvation
on earth
for an angel of God showed him how one
day he might be redeemed.

Ach, könntest du, bleicher Seemann, es
finden! Betet zum Himmel, dass bald
ein Weib Treue ihm halt'!

Ah, wan mariner, could you but find it!
Pray to Heaven that soon
a woman will stay true to him!

**Die Mädchen:**
Ach! könntest du, bleicher Seemann, es
finden! Betet zum Himmel!

**The Maidens:**
Ah, wan mariner, could you but find it!
Pray to Heaven!

**Senta:**
Vor Anker alle sieben Jahr,
ein Weib zu frein, geht er ans Land;
er freite alle sieben Jahr,
noch nie ein treues Weib er fand.
Hui! "Die Segel auf!" Johohe!
Hui! "Den Anker los!" Johohe!
Hui! "Falsche Lieb', falsche Treu'!
Auf, in See, ohne Rast, ohne Ruh!"

**Senta:** *(with ever-increasing agitation)*
Every seven years, he anchor and goes
ashore to woo a wife:
he wooed every seven years,
but never founds a true wife.
Hui! "Hoist sails!" Yohohey!
Hui! "Weigh anchor!" Yohohey!
Hui! "False love, false faith!
Back to sea, without rest or peace!"

*(Senta is overcome by emotion, and sinks back in her chair, seemingly exhausted.*

**Die Mädchen:**
Ach! wo weilt sie, die dir Gottes Engel einst
könnte zeigen?
Wo triffst du sie, die bis in den Tod dein
bleibe treueigen?

**The Maidens:**
Ah, where is she whom the angel of God
someday may show to you?
Where will you meet her who will be your
own true love unto death?

***Senta becomes seized with a sudden inspiration; she springs up from her chair,***
***and solemnly pronounces that the Holländer shall be redeemed: from her true love!***

**Theme of Redemption:**

| | |
|---|---|
| Ich sei's, die dich durch ihre Treu' erlöse! | It is I who will save you with my true love! |
| Mög' Gottes Engel mich dir zeigen! | May God's angel show me to you! |
| Durch mich sollst du das Heil erreichen! | Through me you shall find grace! |

**Mary und Die Mädchen:**
Hilf, Himmel! Senta! Senta!

**Mary and the Maidens:** *(terrified)*
Heaven help us! Senta! Senta!

**Erik:**
Senta! Willst du mich verderben?

**Erik:** *(enters hearing Senta's final words)*
Senta, do you wish to destroy me?

**Die Mädchen:**
Helft, Erik, uns! Sie ist von Sinnen!

**The Maidens:**
Help us, Erik! She's out of her mind!

**Mary:**
Ich fühl in mir das Blut gerinnen!
Abscheulich Bild, du sollst hinaus!
Kommt nur der Vater erst nach Haus!

**Mary:**
I feel my blood curdling!
Horrible portrait, out you go
as soon as her father comes home!

**Erik:**
Der Vater kommt.

**Erik:** *(gloomily)*
Her father's coming now!

**Senta:**
Der Vater kommt?

**Senta:** *(rejoices at the news)*
My father's coming?

**Erik:**
Vom Felsen seh sein Schiff ich nahn.

**Erik:**
From the cliff I saw his ship approaching.

**Die Mädchen:**
Sie sind daheim! Sie sind daheim!

**The Maidens:** *(joyfully)*
They're home! They're home!

**Mary:**
Nun seht, zu was eu'r Treiben frommt!
Im Hause ist noch nichts getan!

**Mary:**
Now see what a fine state we're in!
No work is done in the house yet!

**Die Mädchen:**
Sie sind daheim! Auf, eilt hinaus!

**The Maidens:**
They're home! Hurry, let's go!

**Mary:**
Halt, halt! Ihr bleibet fein im Haus!
Das Schiffsvolk kommt mit leerem Magen.
In Küch' und Keller Säumet nicht!

**Mary:** *(detaining the Maidens)*
Stop! Stop! You just stay indoors!
The crew will come with empty stomachs.
To work in the kitchen and the cellar!

**Die Mädchen:**
Ach! Wie viel hab ich ihn zu fragen!
Ich halte mich vor Neugier nicht!

**The Maidens:**
Oh! I've so much to ask him!
I cannot control my curiosity.

**Mary:**
Lasst euch nur von der Neugier plagen!
Vor allem geht an eure Pflicht!

**Mary:**
You'll have to curb your curiosity —
your duties come first!

**Die Mädchen:**
Schon gut! Sobald nur aufgetragen,
hält hier uns länger keine Pflicht.

**The Maidens:**
All right! Once the food is served,
we'll have no more to do!

*Mary drives the Maidens from the room, and then follows them.*

### Act II — Scene 2
*Senta is at the point of leaving when Erik appears and detains her.*

**Erik:**
Bleib, Senta! Bleib nur einen Augenblick!
Aus meinen Qualen reisse mich! Doch
willst du, ach! so verdirb mich ganz!

**Erik:**                                    *1·12·45*
Stay, Senta! Stay but a moment!
Free me of my torment! Or if you wish,
then destroy me completely!

**Senta:**
Was ist...? Was soll...?

**Senta:** *(hesitantly)*
What is...? What must...?

**Erik:**
O Senta, sprich, was aus mir werden soll?
Dein Vater kommt: eh' wieder er verreist,
wird er vollbringen, was schon oft er wollte.

**Erik:**
Oh, Senta, say, what is to become of me?
Your father is home, before he sails again,
he will do what he has often wanted to.

**Senta:**
Und was meinst du?

**Senta:**
What do you mean?

**Erik:**
Dir einen Gatten geben!

**Erik:**                                    *1·12·25*
Give you to a husband!

Mein Herz, voll Treue bis zum Sterben,
mein dürftig Gut, mein Jägerglück;
darf so um deine Hand ich werben?
Stösst mich dein Vater nicht zurück?
Wenn dann mein Herz im Jammer bricht,
sag, Senta, wer dann für mich spricht?

I offer a heart true unto death,
a few poor possessions, a hunter's lot:
Can I ask for your hand as I am?
Won't your father refuse me?
If then my heart breaks in sorrow,
tell me, Senta, who will speak for me?

*1·12·43*

**Senta:**
Ach, schweige, Erik, jetzt! Lass mich
hinaus, den Vater zu begrüssen!
Wenn nicht, wie sonst, an Bord die Tochter
kommt, wird er nicht zürnen müssen?

**Erik:**
Du willst mich fliehn?

**Senta:**
Ich muss zum Bord.

**Erik:**
Du weichst mir aus!

**Senta:**
Ach, lass mich fort!

**Erik:**
Fliehst du zurück vor dieser Wunde,
die du mir schlugst, dem Liebeswahn?
O, höre mich zu dieser Stunde!
Hör' meine letzte Frage an:
Wenn dieses Herz im Jammer bricht,
wird's Senta sein, die für mich spricht?

**Senta:**
Wie? Zweifelst du an meinem Herzen?
Du zweifelst, ob ich gut dir bin?
O sag, was weckt dir solche Schmerzen?
Was trübt mit Argwohn deinen Sinn?

**Erik:**
Dein Vater, ach! nach Schätzen geizt er nur!
Und Senta, du wie dürft ich auf dich zählen?
Erfülltest du nur eine meiner Bitten?
Kränkst du mein Herz nicht jeden Tag?

**Senta:**
Dein Herz?

**Erik:**
Was soll ich denken! Jenes Bild...

**Senta:**
Das Bild?

**Senta:**
Ah, say no more now, Erik. Let me go out
to greet my father!
If his daughter does not go aboard as usual,
he'll be angry, won't he?

**Erik:**
So you run from me?

**Senta:**
I must go to the harbor.

**Erik:**
You shun me?

**Senta:**
Oh, let me go!

**Erik:**
You shrink from this wound
you gave me, this madness of love?
Oh, listen to me here and now,
hear my last question:
will Senta speaks for me,
if this heart of mine breaks with grief?

**Senta:**
What? You doubt my heart?
You doubt my affection for you?
Tell me, what gives you such pain?
What has made you sad and suspicious?

**Erik:**
Your father, oh, he thinks only of wealth!
You, Senta, how much can I depend on you?
Have you ever granted a wish of mine?
Don't you wound my heart each day?

**Senta:**
Your heart?

**Erik:**
What am I to think? That picture...

**Senta:**
The picture?

**Erik:**
Lasst du von deiner Schwärmerei wohl ab?

**Senta:**
Kann meinem Blick Teilnahme ich verwehren?

**Erik:**
Und die Ballade, heut noch sangst du sie!

**Senta:**
Ich bin ein Kind und weiss nicht, was ich singe!
O sag, wie? Fürchtest du ein Lied, ein Bild?

**Erik:**
Du bist so bleich, sag', sollte ich's nicht
fürchten?

**Senta:**
Soll mich des Ärmsten Schreckenslos nicht
rühren?

**Erik:**
Mein Leiden, Senta, rührt es dich nicht mehr?

**Senta:**
O, prahle nicht! Was kann dein Leiden sein?
Kennst jenes Unglücksel'gen Schicksal du?

Fühlst du den Schmerz, den tiefen Gram,
mit dem herab auf mich er sieht?
Ach, was die Ruhe für ewig ihm nahm,
wie schneidend Weh durchs Herz mir zieht!

**Erik:**
Weh mir! Es mahnt mich mein unsel'ger Traum!
Gott schütze dich! Satan hat dich umgarnt!

**Senta:**
Was erschreckt dich so?

**Erik:**
Senta, lass dir vertraun!
Ein Traum ist's! Hör ihn zur Warnung an!

**Erik:**
Can't you forget your mad infatuation?

**Senta:**
Can I help it if my face shows my pity?

**Erik:**
And you sang the ballad again today!

**Senta:**
I am a child and know not what I sing.
What? Do you fear a song, a picture?

**Erik:**
You are so pale, tell me, Why should I not
fear it?

**Senta:**
Shouldn't I be moved by the poor man's
dreadful fate?

**Erik:**
Doesn't my anguish move you more, Senta?

**Senta:**
Oh, don't boast! What can your anguish be?
Do you know the fate of that unhappy man?
*(Senta leads Erik before the picture)*

Do you feel the pain, the deep grief
with which he looks down on me?
The evil that forever robbed him of his
peace pierces my heart!

**Erik:**
Alas! I recall my hostile dream!
God defend you! Satan has ensnared you!

**Senta:**
What alarms you so?

**Erik:**
Senta! Please believe me:
I had a dream! Heed its warning!

***Senta falls into a chair, exhausted. As Erik begins his narration, she falls into a
trance-like sleep, so that she appears to be dreaming about what is being related to her.***

**Erik:**                                    **Erik:**

Auf hohem Felsen lag ich träumend,
sah unter mir des Meeres Flut;
die Brandung hört'ich, wie sich schäumend
am Ufer brach der Wogen Wut!
Ein fremdes Schiff am nahen Strande
erblickt ich, seltsam, wunderbar;
zwei Männer nahten sich dem Lande,
der ein', ich sah's, dein Vater war.

I lay dreaming on a high cliff,
and saw the angry sea beneath me!
I heard the breakers as the foaming
waters dashed upon the shore, in fury.
I saw a foreign ship near the coast,
strange and mysterious;
two men were coming ashore,
I recognized one as your father.

**Senta:**
Der andre?

**Senta:** *(with eyes closed)*
The other?

**Erik:**
Wohl erkannt ich ihn;
mit schwarzen Wams, bleicher Mien'...

**Erik:**
I knew him well,
with his black jacket, and his pallid face...

**Senta:**
Der düstre Blick...

**Senta:**
and gloomy mien...

**Erik:**
der Seemann, er.

**Erik:** *(pointing to the portrait)*
That sailor, he.

**Senta:**
Und ich?

**Senta:**
And I?

**Erik:**
Du kamst vom Hause her,
du flogst, den Vater zu begrüssen;
doch kaum noch sah ich an dich langen,
du stürztest zu des Fremden Füssen;
ich sah dich seine Knie umfangen...

**Erik:**
You came from the house,
raced to greet your father.
I saw you just as you reached them,
you fell at the stranger's feet,
I saw you clasp his knees...

**Senta:**
Er hub mich auf...

**Senta:** *(with growing excitement)*
He raised me up...

**Erik:**
An seine Brust;
voll Inbrunst hingst du dich an ihn,
du küsstest ihn mit heisser Lust...

**Erik:**
to his breast;
you ardently clung to him
and kissed him with hot passion...

**Senta:**
Und dann?

**Senta:**
And then?

**Erik:**
Sah ich aufs Meer euch fliehn.

**Erik:** *(looking at her in astonishment)*
I saw you both sail away.

**Senta:**
Er sucht mich auf! Ich muss ihn sehn!

**Senta:** *(rising suddenly, enraptured)*
He's looking for me. I must see him!

**Erik:**
Entsetzlich! Mir wird es klar!

**Erik:**
Horrible! It is all clear now!

**Senta:**
Mit ihm muss ich zugrunde gehn!

**Senta:**
I must perish with him!

**Erik:**
Sie ist dahin! mein Traum sprach wahr!

**Erik:**
She is lost! My dream was reality!

*Erik rushes away in despair, terrified. Senta, after her animated outburst,*
*remains deep in silent meditation, with her eyes fixed on the portrait.*

**Senta:**
Ach, möchtest du, bleicher Seemann,
sie finden?
Betet zum Himmel, dass bald
ein Weib Treue ihm...

**Senta:** *(softly but with deep emotion)*
Ah, may you find her, pale seaman!
Pray to Heaven that soon
a woman will be true to you...

*Daland and the Holländer appear at the door.*

### Act II — Scene 3
*Senta's gaze sweeps from the portrait to the Holländer. After a cry of astonishment,*
*she becomes spellbound, unable to take her eyes from him.*
*Likewise, the Holländer becomes transfixed on Senta.*

**Daland:**
Mein Kind, du siehst mich auf der Schwelle:
Wie? Kein Umarmen? Keinen Kuss?
Du bleibst gebannt an deiner Stelle:
Verdien ich, Senta, solchen Gruss?

**Daland:**
My child, I am here at our threshold.
What? No embrace? No kiss?
You stand as if you are bewitched.
Senta, do I deserve such a greeting?

**Senta:**
Gott dir zum Gruss!
Mein Vater, sprich!
Wer ist der Fremde?

**Senta:** *(grasping Daland's hand)*
God greet you!
Father, tell me,
who is the stranger?

**Daland:**
Drängst du mich?

**Daland:** *(laughing)*
You really want to know?

Mögst du, mein Kind, den fremden Mann
willkommen heissen! Seemann ist er, gleich
mir, das Gastrecht spricht er an.
Lang ohne Heimat, stets auf fernen, weiten
Reisen, in fremden Landen er der Schätze
viel gewann.
Aus seinem Vaterland verwiesen,
für einen Herd er reichlich lohnt.
Sprich, Senta, würd es dich verdriessen,
wenn dieser Fremde bei uns wohnt?

My child, bid this stranger welcome!
He is a seaman like me, who asks to be our
guest.
Long homeless,
always sailing far and wide,
he has won rich treasure in foreign lands.
As an exile from his homeland,
he'll pay well for a hearth.
Tell me, Senta, would it vex you
if this stranger lodged with us? ⌐

*After Senta nods her assent, Daland turns to address the Holländer.*

Sagt, hab ich sie zuviel gepreisen?
Ihr seht sie selbst, ist sie euch recht?
Soll ich von Lob noch überfliessen?
Gesteht, sie zieret ihr Geschlect?

Now, was my I praise excessive?
You see her yourself, do you approve?
Do I need to lavish more praise?
Admit it, she adorns her sex!    ⌐

*The Holländer makes a gesture of assent. Daland then turns to Senta.*

Mögst du, mein Kind, dem Manne
freundlich dich erweisen; von deinem
Herzen auch spricht holde Gab er an;
reich ihm die Hand, denn Bräutigam sollst
du ihn heissen! Stimmst du der Vater bei, ist
morgen er dein Mann.

Will you, my child, be friendly to this man?
He seeks too gracious a gift from your heart:
if you give him your hand,
you shall call him your bridegroom,
and if you agree with your father,
tomorrow he shall be your husband.

*Senta responds convulsively, her demeanor expressing anxiety.*
*Daland produces some jewelry which he shows to Senta.*

Sieh dieses Band, sieh diese Spangen!
Was er besitzt, macht dies gering.
Muss, teures Kind, dich's nicht verlangen?
Dein ist es, wechselst du den Ring.

Look at this bracelet, these clasps!
This is nothing to what he owns.
Surely you want them, dear child?
It is all yours when you exchange rings.

*Senta and the Holländer remain spellbound; neither one pays attention to Daland.*

Doch keines spricht! Sollt' ich hier lästig
sein? So ist's! Am besten lass' ich sie allein.

But neither speaks. Do I intrude?
Yes. Better leave them alone.

Mögst du den edlen Mann gewinnen!
Glaub mir, solch Glück wird nimmer neu!

*(to Senta)*
May you win this fine man!
Believe me, such luck never comes twice.

Bleibt hier allein! Ich geh von hinnen:
Glaubt mir, wie schön, so ist sie treu!

*(to the Holländer)*
Stay here alone! I'm leaving.
Believe me, she is as true as she is fair.

*Daland departs slowly, leaving Senta and the Holländer alone.*
*Both remain rapt in contemplation of one another.*

**Holländer:**
Wie aus der Ferne längst vergangner Zeiten
spricht dieses Mädchens Bild zu mir:
wie ich's geträumt seit bangen Ewigkeiten,
vor meinen Augen seh ich's hier.

**Holländer:** *(deeply moved)*
This maiden's image speaks to me, as if out
of the mist of times long gone:
I see her now before my eyes,
just as I dreamed of her through the ages.

Wohl hub auch ich voll Sehnsucht meine
Blicke
aus tiefer Nacht empor zu einem Weib:
ein schlagend Herz liess, ach! mir Satans Tücke,
dass eingedenk ich meiner Qualen bleib.
Die düstre Glut, die hier ich fühle brennen,
sollt ich Unseliger sie Liebe nennen?
Ach nein! Die Sehnsucht ist es nach dem
Heil: würd es durch solchen Engel mir zuteil!

I have often lifted my eyes,
at the dead of night,
longing for a wife.
To remind me of my torment, Satan's
revenge left me but a pounding heart.
The dull glow that I feel burning here,
can I, in my misery, call it love?
Ah, no! It is my yearning for redemption:
that has become fulfilled through this angel!

**Senta:**
Versank ich jetzt in wunderbares Träumen?
Was ich erblicke, ist's ein Wahn?
Weilt' ich bisher in trügerischen Räumen?
Brach des Erwachens Tag heut an?
Er steht vor mir, mit leidenvollen Zügen,
es spricht sein unerhörter Gram zu mir:
kann tiefen Mitleids Stimme mich belügen?

**Senta:**
Am I deep in a wonderful dream?
What I see, is it mere fancy?
Have I been in some false world till now,
is my day of awakening dawning?
He stands before me, his face lined with
suffering, and revealing his terrible grief to
me: can intense pity's voice lie to me?

Wie ich ihn oft gesehn, so steht er hier.
Die Schmerzen, die in meinem Busen
brennen, ach, dies Verlangen, wie soll ich es
nennen?
Wonach mit Sehnsucht es dich treibt, das
Heil, würd es, du Ärmster, dir durch mich
zuteil!

Here he stands,
as I have often seen him,
The pain that burns within my breast,
ah, this compassion, how shall I call it?
What you yearn for, salvation,
would it come true, poor man,
through me!

**Holländer:**
Wirst du des Vaters Wahl nicht schelten?
Was er versprach, wie, dürft es gelten?
Du könntest dich für ewig mir ergeben,
und deine Hand dem Fremdling reichtest
du?
Soll finden ich, nach qualenvollen Leben
in deiner Treu' die langersehnte Ruh?

**Holländer:** *(drawing closer to Senta)*
Do you agree with your father's choice?
What he promised, say,
can I count on it?
Could you offer your hand to a stranger,
and give yourself to me for ever?
Shall I, after a life of anguish, find my long-
sought redemption in your loyalty?

**Senta:**
Wer du auch seist, und welches das
Verderben, dem grausam dich dein Schicksal
konnte weih, was auch das Los, das ich
mir sollt' erwerben,
gehorsam stests werd ich dem Vater sein!

**Senta:**
Whoever you are, whatever the evil
that cruel fate has meted out to you,
and whatever the future holds in store for
me,
I shall always obey my father!

**Holländer:**
So unbedingt, wie? könnte dich urchdringen
für meine Leiden tiefstes Mitgefühl?

**Holländer:**
What? So unhesitating? Have you
such deep pity for my suffering?

**Senta:**
O, welche Leiden? Könnt ich Trost dir
bringen!

**Senta:** *(aside)*
Oh, what suffering! Could I but console
you!

**Holländer:**
Welch holder Klang im nächtigen Gewühl!

**Holländer:** *(overhearing her)*
What a sweet sound amid the murky tumult!

Du bist ein Engel, eines Engels Liebe
Verworfne selbst zu trösten weiss!
Ach, wenn Erlösung mir zu hoffen bliebe,
Allewiger, durch diese sei's!

You are an angel! An angel's love
can comfort even a lost soul!
Ah, if I can still hope for redemption,
eternal God, may it come through her!

**Senta:**
Ach, wenn Erlösung ihm zu hoffen bliebe,
Allewiger, durch mich nur sei's!

**Senta:**
Ah, if he can still hope for redemption,
Eternal God, may it come through me!

**Holländer:**
Ach, könntest das Geschick du ahnen,
dem dann mit mir du angehörst,
dich würd es an das Opfer mahnen,
das du mir bringst, wenn Treu' du schwörst:
Es flöhe schaudernd deine Jugend
dem Lose, dem du sie willst weihn,
nennst du des Weibes schönste Tugend,
nennst ew'ge Treue du nicht dein!

**Holländer:**
Ah, if you realized the fate
that you would then be sharing with me,
it would alert you of the sacrifice
you make for me, if you swear to be true to me.
Your young soul would flee in horror
from the ruin to which you condemn it,
without woman's noblest virtue,
without eternal fidelity.

**Senta:**
Wohl kenn ich Weibes heil'ge Pflichten;
sei drum gestrost, unsel'ger Mann!
Lass über die das Schicksal richten,
die seinem Spruche trotzen kann!
In meines Herzens höchster Reine
kenn ich der Treue Hochgebot.
Wem ich sie weih, schenk ich die eine;
die Treue bis zum Tod.

**Senta:**
I know well a woman's sacred duty,
take heart, then, unhappy man!
Let destiny judge me
who can defy its sentence!
In the sheer purity of my heart
I know what loyalty demands most.
To whom I show it, I give it all,
true love till death!

**Holländer:**

Ein heil'ger Balsam meinen Wunden
dem Schwur, dem hohen Wort entfliesst.
Hört es: mein Heil hab ich gefunden,
ihr Mächte, die ihr zurück mich stiesst!
Du, Stern des Unheils, sollst erblassen!
Licht meiner Hoffnung, leuchte neu!
Ihr Engel, die mich einst verlassen,
stärkt jetzt dies Herz in seiner Treu!

**Senta:**

Von mächt'gem Zauber überwunden,
reisst mich's zu seiner Rettung fort;
hier habe Heimat er gefunden,
hier ruh sein Schiff in sichrem Port!

**Holländer:** *(in exaltation)*

A holy balm for my wounds
springs from this solemn oath.
Hear me: I have found my deliverance,
you powers that have repulsed me!
The star of my evil fate shall fail,
shine anew, light of my hope!
You angels who once abandoned me,
strengthen the fate in this heart!

**Senta:**

By overcoming mysterious magic,
I am swept to his rescue:
here may he find a home,
may his ship anchor in our safe port!

Was ist's, das mächtig in mir lebet?
Was schliesst berauscht mein Busen ein?
Allmächt'ger, was so hoch mich erhebet,
lass es die Kraft der Treue sein!

What stirs so strongly within me?
What fills my heart with rapture?
Almighty God, may the source of my
exaltation be the strength of my true love.

*1:48:03*

**Daland:**

Verzeiht! Mein Volk hält draussen sich nicht
mehr;
nach jeder Rückkunft, wisset, gibt's ein
Fest:
verschönern möcht ich's, komme deshalb
her,
ob mit Verlobung sich's vereinen lässt?

Ich denk, ihr habt nach Herzenswunsch
gefreit?

Senta, mein Kind sag, bist auch du bereit?

**Daland:** *(reappears)*

Forgive me! My people, I will stay outside
no longer.
After each voyage, you know, we have a
feast.
To grace the occasion, I have come to ask
if you agree to the betrothal?

*(to the Holländer)*
I think you courted to your heart's desire?

*(to Senta)*
Senta, my child, say, are you willing?

**Senta:**

Hier meine Hand! Und ohne Reu'
bis in den Tod gelob ich Treu'!

**Senta:** *(with solemn resolution)*

Here is my hand! And without regret
till death I vow to be true!

**Holländer:**

Sie reicht die Hand! Gesprochen sei Hohn,
Hölle, dir! Hohn, Hölle, dir durch ihre Treu'!

**Holländer:**

She gives her hand! Hell, you have been
mocked, by her true love!

**Daland:**
Euch soll dies Bündnis nicht gereun!
Zum Fest! Heut soll sich alles freun!

**Daland:**
You will not regret this union!
To the feast! Today shall everyone rejoice!

**END of ACT II**

## Act III — Scene 1

*A cove with a rocky beach. On one side, Daland's house.*
*In the background, the Norwegian and The Flying Dutchman*
*ships are moored close to one another.*
*It is a clear night. The Norwegian sailors are merry-making on the deck.*
*In sinister contrast, The Flying Dutchman is shrouded in unnatural gloom*
*and deathly silence.*

**Norwegischen Matrosen:**                                    **Norwegian Sailors:**

*1:49:30*
*USE OF CHORUS*

Steuermann! Lass die Wacht!                     Steersman, leave your watch!
Steuermann! Her zu uns!                          Steersman, join us!
Ho! He! Je! Ha!                                  Ho! Hey! Je! Ha!
Hisst die Segel auf! Anker fest!                 Hoist the sails! Anchor fast!
Steuermann, her!                                 Steersman, here!
Fürchten weder Wind noch bösen Strand,           We fear no wind nor treacherous coast.
wollen heute mal recht lustig sein!              Today we'll be right and merry!

Jeder hat sein Mädel auf dem Land,               Each has his girl ashore,
herrlichen Tabak und guten Branntwein.           grand tobacco and good brandy!
Hussassahe!                                      Hussassahey!
Klipp' und Sturm' drauss                         Rocks and storms outside
Jollohohe!                                       yollohohey!
lachen wir aus!                                  we laugh at them!
Hussassahe!                                      Hussassahey!

Segel ein! Anker fest!                           Furl sails! Anchor fast!
Klipp' und Sturm lachen wir aus!                 Rocks and storms we laugh at them!
Steuermann, lass die Wacht!                      Steersman, leave your watch!
Steuermann, her zu uns!                          Steersman, join us!
Ho! He! Je! Ha!                                  Ho! Hey! Ye! Ha!
Steuermann, her! Trink mit uns!                  Steersman, drink with us!
Ho! He! Je! Ha!                                  Ho! Hey! Ye! Ha!
Klipp' und Sturm, he!                            Rocks and storms, hey!
sind vorbei, he!                                 are over, hey!
Hussahe! Hallohe!                                Hussahey! Hallohey!
Hussahe! Steuermann, He!                         Hussahey! Steersman! Ho!
Her! Komm und trink mit uns!                     Here, come and drink with us!

*The Norwegian sailors dance about the deck, accompanying the down-beat of each bar*
*with heavy foot-stamping.*

**Die Mädchen:**
Mein! Seht doch an! Sie tanzen gar!
Der Mädchen bedarf's da nicht, fürwahr!

**Norwegischen Matrosen:**
He! Mädel! Halt! Wo geht ihr hin?

**Die Mädchen:**
Steht euch nach frischem Wein der Sinn?
Eu'r Nachbar dort soll auch was haben!
Ist Trank und Speis' für euch allein?

**Steuermann:**
Fürwahr! Tragt's hin den armen Knaben!
Vor Durst sie scheinen matt zu sein!

**Norwegischen Matrosen:**
Man hört sie nicht!

**Steuermann:**
Ei, seht doch nur!
Kein Licht, von der Mannschaft keine Spur!

**Die Mädchen:**
He! Seeleut'! He! Wollt Fackeln ihr?
Wo seid ihr doch? Man sieht nicht hier!

**Norwegischen Matrosen:**
Hahaha! Weckt sie nicht auf! Sie schlafen
noch.

**Die Mädchen:**
He! Seeleut'! He! Antwortet doch!

**Norwegischen Matrosen:**
Haha! Wahrhaftig, sie sind tot;
sie haben Speis' und Trank nicht not!

**Die Mädchen:**
Ei, Seeleute, liegt ihr so faul schon im Nest?
Ist heute für euch denn nicht auch ein Fest?

**Norwegischen Matrosen:**
Sie liegen fest auf ihrem Platz,
wie Drachen hüten sie den Schatz!

**The Maidens:** *(with food and drink)*
Well! Just look! Dancing, indeed!
They don't seem to need us girls!

*(The Maidens head to the Holländer's ship)*
**Norwegian Sailors:**
Hey! Girls! Stop! Where are you going?

**The Maidens:**
You've a taste for cool wine?
Your neighbor's there shall have some too!
Is the food and drink for you alone?

**Steersman:**
Right! Take it to the poor lads!
They must be faint from thirst!

**Norwegian Sailors:**
We can't hear them.

**Steersman:**
Oh, just look!
No light! No sign of the crew!

**The Maidens:** *(just about to board)*
Hey! Sailors! Do you want torches?
Where are you? We see nothing.

**Norwegian Sailors:** *(laughing)*
Hahaha! Don't wake them up! They're still
asleep!

**The Maidens:** *(shouting to the ship)*
Hey! Sailors! Hey! Answer then!

**Norwegian Sailors:** *(mockingly)*
Haha! Truly, they are dead:
they have no need of food and drink!

**The Maidens:**
Hey, Sailors, are you already lying snug in
your bunks? No feasting for you today?

**Norwegian Sailors:**
They're lying low, sitting tight,
like dragons guarding their treasure!

**Die Mädchen:**
He! Seeleute, wollt ihr nicht frischen Wein?
Ihr müsset wahrlich doch durstig auch sein!

**The Maidens:**
Hey, sailors! Don't you want some wine?
Surely you must be thirsty, too!

**Norwegischen Matrosen:**
Sie trinken nicht, sie singen nicht!
In ihrem Schiffe brennt kein Licht.

**Norwegian Sailors:**
They don't drink, they don't sing;
no light burns on their ship.

**Die Mädchen:**
Sagt, habt ihr denn nicht auch ein Schätzen
am Land? Wollt ihr nicht mit tanzen auf
freundlichen Strand?

**The Maidens:**
Say! Haven't you sweethearts ashore?
Don't you want to dance with them
on the pleasant beach?

**Norwegischen Matrosen:**
Sie sind schon alt und bleich statt rot,
und ihre Liebsten, die sind tot!

**Norwegian Sailors:**
They must be old and pale, not red-blooded!
and their sweethearts are dead!

**Die Mädchen:**
He! Seeleut'! Seeleut'! Wacht doch auf!
Wir bringen euch Speis' und Trank zuhauf!

**The Maidens:** *(calling loudly)*
Hey! Sailors! Sailors! Wake up!
We bring you food and drink in plenty!

**Norwegischen Matrosen:**
He! Seeleut'! Seeleut'! Wacht doch auf!

**Norwegian Sailors:**
Hey! Sea mates! Sea mates! Wake up!

**Die Mädchen:**
Wahrhaftig, ja! Sie scheinen tot!
Sie haben Speis' und Trank nicht not.

**The Maidens:** *(fearful after a long silence)*
Yes, it is true! They seem dead.
They've no need of food and drink.

**Norwegischen Matrosen:**
Vom fliegenden Holländer wisst ihr ja:
Sein Schiff, wie es liebt, wie es lebt, seht ihr da!

**Norwegian Sailors:** *(cheerfully)*
You know of the Flying Dutchman!
The ship you see there is exactly like his!

**Die Mädchen:**
So weckt die Mannschaft ja nicht auf!
Gespenster sind's, wir schwören drauf!

**The Maidens:**
Then don't wake the crew;
they are ghosts, we swear!

**Norwegischen Matrosen:**
Wieviel hundert Jahre schon sied ihr zur
See? Euch tut ja der Sturm und die Klippe
nicht weh!

**Norwegian Sailors:**
How many centuries
have you been at sea?
Storms and rocks can do you no harm!

**Die Mädchen:**
Sie trinken nicht, sie singen nicht,
in ihrem Schiffe brennt kein Licht.

**The Maidens:**
They don't drink! They don't sing!
No light burns on their ship!

**Norwegischen Matrosen:**
Habt ihr keine Brief', keine Aufträg' für's
Land? Unsern Urgrossvätern wir bringen's
zur Hand!

**Norwegian Sailors:**
Have you any letters or news to tell people
ashore? We'll deliver them to our great-
grandfathers!

**Die Mädchen:**
Sie sind schon alt und bleich statt rot,
und ihre Liebsten, ach! sind tot!

**Norwegischen Matrosen:**
Hei, Seeleute, spannt eure Segel doch auf,
und zeigt uns des fliegenden Holländers Lauf!

**Die Mädchen:**
Sie hören nicht! Uns graust es hier!
Sie wollen nichts, was rufen wir?

**Norwegischen Matrosen:**
Ihr Mädel, lasst die Toten ruhn!
Lasst's uns Lebend'gen gütlich tun!

**Die Mädchen:**
So nehmt! Der Nachbar hat's verschmäht!

**Steuermann:**
Wie? Kommt ihr denn nicht selbst an Bord?

**Norwegischen Matrosen:**
Wie? Kommt ihr denn nicht selbst an Bord?

**Die Mädchen:**
Ei, jetzt noch nicht! Es ist ja nicht spät!
Wir kommen bald, jetzt trinkt nur fort!
Und wenn ihr wollt, so tanzt dazu,
nor gönnt dem müden Nachbar Ruh!

**Norwegischen Matrosen:**
Jucche! Da gibt's die Fülle!
Lieb Nachbar, habe Dank!

**Steuermann:**
Zum Rand sein Glas ein jeder fülle!
Lieb Nachbar liefert uns den Trank.

**Norwegischen Matrosen:**
Hallohohoho! Hallohohoho!
Lieb' Nachbarn, habt ihr Stimm und Sprach,
so wachet auf und macht's uns nach!

**The Maidens:**
They must be old and pale, not red-blooded!
And their sweethearts, alas, are dead!

**Norwegian Sailors:** *(noisily)*
Hey, sea mates! Set your sails
and show us the Flying Dutchman's speed!

**The Maidens:** *(frightened, retreating)*
They don't hear! Gives you the creeps!
They want nothing, so why call to them?

**Norwegian Sailors:**
You girls, let the dead rest!
Let us, the living, enjoy ourselves!

**The Maidens:** *(handing them a basket)*
Here! Your neighbor has spurned it.

**Steersman:**
What? Aren't you coming aboard?

**Norwegian Sailors:**
What? Aren't you coming aboard?

**The Maidens:**
Oh, not just yet! It's not late.
We'll come back soon. You drink up,
but if you want to dance as well,
let your weary neighbors rest!

**Norwegian Sailors:** *(opening the baskets)*
Hurrah! There's plenty here!
Dear neighbors, thank you!

**Steersman:**
Everyone fill his glass to the brim!
Our good neighbors send us drink!

**Norwegian Sailors:**
Hallohohoho! Hallohohoho!
Good neighbors, if you've voice and
speech, wake up and follow our example!

*There is a faint sign of life aboard the Holländer's ship.*

**Norwegischen Matrosen:**
Wachet auf! Wachet auf!
Auf! macht's uns nach!

**Norwegian Sailors:** *(laughing)*
Wake up! Wake up!
Up and follow our example!

*The Norwegian sailors noisily clink their drinking cups.*

Hussa!
Steuermann! Lass die Wacht!
Steuermann, her zu uns!
Ho, he, je, ha!
Hisst die Segel auf! Anker fest!
Steuermann, her!

Hussa!
Steersman, leave your watch!
Steersman, join us!
Ho! Hey! Ye! Ha!
Hoist the sails! Anchor fast!
Steersman, here!

*1:58:43*

Wachten manche Nacht bei Sturm und Graus,
tranken oft des Meers gesalznes Nass;
heute wachen wir bei Saus und Schmaus,
besseres Getränk gibt Mädel uns vom Fass.
Hussassahe! Klipp' und Sturm drauss.
Jollolohe! lachen wir aus!

We watched many a night in storm and terror,
we often drank the sea's brine:
today we watch, carousing and feasting,
the girls giving us better drink from the cask.
Hussassahey! Rocks and storms, outside!
Yollohohey! We laugh at them!

Hussassahe! Segel ein! Anker fest!
Klipp' und Sturm lachen wir aus!
Steuermann, lass die Wacht!
Steuermann, her zu uns!
Ho, he, je, ha!
Steuermann, her! Trink mit uns!
Klipp' und Sturm, ha!
sind vorbei! He!
Hussahe! Hallohe!
Hussahe! Steuermann! He!
Ho! He! Je! Ha!
Her, komm und trink mit uns!

Hussassahey! Furl sails! Anchor fast!
Rocks and storms we laugh at them!
Steersman, leave your watch!
Steersman, join us!
Ho! Hey! Ye! Ha!
Steersman, here! Drink with us!
Rocks and storms, ha!
are over, hey!
Hussahey! Hallohey!
Hussahey! Steersman! Ho!
Ho! Hey! Ye! Ha!
Here, come and drink with us!

*The sea is calm all over, except near the Holländer's ship, where it has begun to rise.*
*A dull blue flame flares up like a watchfire. A storm wind whistles through the rigging.*
*The crew of The Flying Dutchman, hitherto invisible, begins to stir about the ship.*

**Die Mannschaft des Holländers:**
Johohoe! Johohohoe!
Hojohohoe! Hoe! Hoe! Hoe!
Huissa!
Nach dem Land treibt der Sturm,
Huissa!
Segel ein! Anker los!
Huissa!
In die Bucht laufet ein!
Schwarzer Hauptmann, geh ans Land!
Sieben Jahre sind vorbei!

**The Flying Dutchman's Crew:**
Yohohoeh! Yohohohoeh!
Hojohohoeh! Hoeh! Hoeh! Hoeh!
Huissa!
The storms sweep ashore,
Huissa!
Furl sails! Anchor away!
Huissa!
Run for the bay!
Somber capitain, go ashore,
the seven years are over!

Frei' um blonden Mädchens Hand!
Blondes Mädchen, sie ihm treu!
Lustig heut, hui!
Bräutigam! Hui!
Sturmwind heult Brautmusik, Ozean tanzt dazu!
Hui! Horch, er pfeift!
Kapitän! Bist wieder da?
Hui! Segel auf!

Deine Braut, sag, wo sie blieb?
Hui! Auf, in See!
Kapitän! Kapitän! hast kein Glück in der Lieb'! Hahaha!
Sause, Sturmwind, heule zu!
Unsern Sgeln lässt du Ruh!
Satan hat sie uns gefeit,
reissen nicht in Ewigkeit,
hohoe! Hoe! Nicht in Ewigkeit!

Seek the fair maid's hand!
Fair maid, be true to him!
Be merry today, hui!
A bridegroom, hui!
The stormwind howls, bridal-music and the ocean dances to it!
Hui! Hark, he whistles!
Captain, here again?
Hui! Hoist sail!

But your bride, say, where is she?
Hui! Back to sea!
Captain! Captain! You're unlucky in love! Hahaha!
Scream, storm wind, howl!
Leave our sails alone!
Satan has blessed them,
and they will not rend.
Hohoeh! Hoeh! Never!

*The Flying Dutchman tosses back and forth in the raging waters,*
*a gale howling through the rigging. Yet, everywhere else, the sea and sky are calm.*
*The Norwegian sailors have watched and listened in astonishment, then with terror.*

**Norwegischen Matrosen:**
Welcher Sang! Ist es Spuk?
Wie mich's graust!
Stimmet an unser Lied! Singet laut!

Steuermann, lass die Wacht!...

**Norwegian Sailors:**
What a shanty! Are they spooks?
Makes the flesh shiver!
Strike up our song! Sing it loud!

Steersman, leave your watch!....

**Die Mannschaft des Holländers:**
Huissa!
Johohoe! Johohoe!
Sause, Sturmwind, heule zu!....

**The Flying Dutchman's Crew:**
Huissa!
Yohohoeh! Yohohohoeh!
Scream, storm-wind, howl!....

*Sinister cries from The Flying Dutchman's crew silences the Norwegian sailors;*
*they become terrified, leave the deck, and go below while making the sign of the Cross.*
*The ghostly crew bursts into mocking laughter, whereupon gloom and silence*
*once more envelop their ship and the surrounding sea.*

### Act III — Scene 3

*Senta appears in great agitation as she hurries from the house, followed by Erik.*

**Erik:**
Was musst' ich hören! Gott, was musst' ich
sehen! Ist's Täuschung? Wahrheit? Ist es Tat?

**Senta:**
O frage nicht! Antwort darf ich nicht geben.

**Erik:**
Gerechter Gott! Kein Zweifel, es ist wahr!
Welch unheilvolle Macht riss dich dahin?
Welche Gewalt verführte dich so schnell,
grausam zu brechen dieses treuste Herz!

Dein Vater, ha! den Bräut'gam bracht er mit;
wohl kenn ich ihn, mir ahnte, was geschieht!
Doch du, ist's möglich! reichest deine Hand
dem Mann, der deine Schwelle kaum betrat.

**Senta:**
Nicht wieter! Schweig! Ich muss! ich muss!

**Erik:**
O des Gehorsams, blind wie deine Tat!
Den Wink des Vaters nanntest du willkommen,
mit einem Stoss vernichtest du mein Herz!

**Senta:**
Nicht mehr! nicht mehr! Ich darf dich nicht
mehr seh'n,
nicht an dich denken: hohe Pflicht gebeut's!

**Erik:**
Welch hohe Pflicht? Ist's höhre nich, zu
halten,
was du mir einst gelobtest, ewige Treue?

**Senta:**
Wie? Ew'ge Treue hätt' ich dir gelobt?

**Erik:**
Senta, o Senta, leugnest du?

**Erik:**
What I heard! God, what I saw!
Is it an illusion? The truth? A fact?

**Senta:** *(turning away, painfully moved)*
Oh, do not ask! I dare not answer!

**Erik:**
Merciful God! It is true beyond doubt.
What unholy power tore you from me?
What force seduced you so rapidly,
to cruelly break this truest of hearts?

Your father, ha, he brought the bridegroom;
I know him well, I expected this to happen!
But you, is it possible, offer your hand to a
man who has hardly crossed your threshold!

**Senta:** *(struggling with herself)*
No more! Say no more! I must, I must!

**Erik:**
Oh, this obedience, this blind behavior!
You welcomed your father's suggestion,
and with one blow broke my heart!

*DIS SFSSOL*

**Senta:** *(agitated)*
No more! No more! I must never see you
again,
nor think of you: a noble duty decrees it.

**Erik:**
What noble duty? Isn't it nobler to keep
your vow of eternal love that you once
made to me?

**Senta:** *(frightened)*
What? I vowed to always be true to you?

**Erik:** *(sorrowfully)*
Senta, oh Senta, you deny it?

Andante
ERIK

Willst je - nes Tag's du nicht dich mehr ent - sin - nen,

Willst jenes Tags du nicht dich mehr
entsinnen, als du zu dir mich riefest in das
Tal? Als, dir des Hochlands Blume zu
gewinnen, mutvoll ich trug Beschwerden
ohne Zahl?

Don't you remember that day
when you called me
to join you in the valley?
When I bravely took countless risks to get
highland flowers for you?

Gedenkst du, wie auf steilem Felsenriffe
vom Ufer wir den Vater scheiden sahn?
Er zog dahin auf weissbeschwingtem
Schiffe, und meinem Schutz vertraute er
dich an. Als sich dein Arm um meinen
Nacken schlang,
gestandest du mir Liebe nicht aufs neu?

Do you recall when we were on a steep cliff
and you saw your father leave the shore?
He sailed on a white-winged ship, and he
had entrusted you to my protection.
And when you wrapped your arms around
my neck, didn't you declare your love
anew?

Was bei der Hände Druck mich hehr
durchdrang
sag, war's nicht Versichrung deiner Treu'?

That rapture that I felt from the touch of
your hand, wasn't that assurance of your
true love?

*The Holländer has overheard Senta and Erik and wildly rushes toward them.*

**Holländer:**
Verloren! Ach! Verloren! Ewig verlornes Heil!

**Holländer:**
Lost! Ah, lost! Redemption lost forever!

**Erik:**
Was seh ich! Gott!

**Erik:** *(recoiling in terror)*
What do I see? God!

**Holländer:**
Senta, leb wohl!

**Holländer:**
Senta, farewell!

**Senta:**
Halt ein! Unsel'ger!

**Senta:** *(barring his way)*
Wait, unhappy man!

**Erik:**
Was beginnst du?

**Erik:** *(to Senta)*
What are you going to do?

**Holländer:**
In See! In See! In See für ew'ge Zeiten!

**Holländer:**
To sea! To sea! Forever!

Um deine Treue ist's getan,
um deine Treue, um mein Heil!
Leb wohl! Ich will dich nicht verderben!

*(to Senta)*
Your pledge is ended,
and with your pledge, my hope of grace!
Farewell, I shall not destroy you!

**Erik:**
Entsetzlich! Dieser Blick!

**Erik:**
Horrible! That look in his eyes!

**Senta:**
Halt' ein! Von dannen sollst du nimmer fliehn!

**Senta:** *(restraining the Holländer)*
Wait! You shall never flee from here!

**Holländer:**
Segel auf! Anker los!
Sagt Lebewohl auf Ewigkeit dem lande!
Fort auf das Meer triebt's mich auf's neue!
Ich zweifl an dir! Ich zweifl an Gott!
Dahin, dahin, ist alle Treue!
Was du gelobtest, war dir Spott!

**Holländer:** *(blasting his whistle)*
Hoist sails! Weigh anchor!
Say farewell to land forever!
I'm driven again to sea!
I doubt you just as I doubt God!
Dead, all faith is dead!
Your promise was frivolous!

**Senta:**
Ha, zweifelst du an meiner Treue?
Unsel'ger, was verblendet dich?
Halt ein! Das Bündnis nicht bereue!
Was ich gelobte, halte ich!

**Senta:**
Ha! do you doubt my true love?
Stay! Do not regret our bond!
What I promised,
I shall fulfill!

**Erik:**
Was hör ich! Gott, was muss ich sehen?
Muss ich dem Ohr, dem Auge traun?
Senta! Willst du zugrunde gehen?
Zu mir! Du bist in Satans Klau'n!

**Erik:**
What do I hear! God, what is this I see?
Am I to trust my ears, my eyes?
Senta! Do you want to perish?
Come to me! You are in Satan's clutches!

**Holländer:**
Erfahre das Geschick, vor dem ich dich
bewahr'!
Verdammt bin ich zum grässlichsten der
Lose; zehnfacher Tod wär mir erwünschte
Lust! Vom Fluch ein Weib allein mich kann
erlösen, ein Weib, das Treu' bis in den Tod
mir hält.

**Holländer:**
Hear the destiny from which I defend you!
I am condemned to the most ghastly fate,
from which a ten-fold death
would be a long awaited joy!
A woman alone
can free me from the curse:
a woman true to me till death.

Wohl hast du Treue mir gelobt, doch vor
dem Ewigen noch nicht; dies rettet dich!
Denn wiss', Unsel'ge, welches das
Geschick, das jene trifft, die mir die Treue
brechen: Ew'ge Verdammnis ist ihr Los!
Zahllose Opfer fielen diesem Spruch
durch mich: Du aber sollst gerettet sein!
Leb wohl!
Fahr him, mein Heil, in Ewigkeit!

You did vow to be true, but
not solemnly before God: this saves you!
For know, poor girl, the fate that awaits
those who break their faith with me,
is eternal damnation!
Countless victims have paid this penalty
through me! But you shall be saved.
Farewell!
Farewell for ever to my salvation!

**Erik:**
Zu Hilfe! Rettet, rettet sie!

**Erik:** *(terrified, calls the house and ship)*
Help! Save, oh, save her!

**Senta:**
Wohl kenn ich dich! Wohl kenn ich dein
Geschick!
Ich kannte dich, als ich zuerst dich sah!
Das Ende deiner Qual ist da: Ich bin's,
durch deren Treu' dein Heil du finden sollst!

**Senta:** *(scrutinizing the Holländer)*
I know you well! And well I know your
fate!
I knew you when first I saw you!
The end of your torment is near! I am she
by whose true love you shall find salvation!

**Erik:**
Helft ihr! Sie ist verloren!

**Erik:**
Help her! She is lost!

*At Erik's cry for help, Daland, Mary and the Maidens hurry from the house,*
*followed by Norwegian sailors from their ship.*

**Mary, Daland, Mädchen, Matrosen:**
Was erblick ich!

**Mary, Daland, Maidens, Sailors:**
What do I see!

**Holländer:**
Du kennst mich nicht, du ahnst nicht, wer
ich bin!

**Holländer:** *(to Senta)*
You do not know me, and you cannot guess
who I am!

*The Holländer points to his ship, The Flying Dutchman; its red sails are unfurled,*
*and its crew, in ghostly activity, prepares for departure.*

Befrag die Meere aller Zonen, befrag
den Seemann, der den Ozean durchstrich:
er kennt dies Schiff, das Schrecken aller
Frommen:
den fliegenden Holländer nennt man mich.

Ask the seas around the globe,
ask the seaman who has sailed the ocean.
he knows this ship, the terror of all devout
men:
they call me the Flying Dutchman!

*The Holländer rushes aboard his ship, which instantly heads out to sea.*
*Senta tries to follow him but is held back by Daland and Erik.*

**Die Mannschaft des Holländers:**
Johohoe! Johohohoe! Hojohohoe!
Hoe! Hoe! Hoe! Huissa!

**Crew of the Flying Dutchman:**
Yohohoeh! Yohohohoeh! Hojohohoeh!
Hoeh! Hoeh! Hoeh! Huissa!

**Mary, Daland, Erik, Mädchen, Matrosen:**
Senta! Senta! Was willst du tun?

**Mary, Daland, Erik, Maidens, Sailors:**
Senta! Senta! What are you doing?

*Senta tears herself free, and rushes to a rock overhanging the sea,*
*from where she calls after the departing ship, The Flying Dutchman.*

**Senta:**
Preis deinen Engel und sein Gebot!
Hier steh ich, treu dir bis zum Tod!

**Senta:**
Praise your angel and his proclamation!
Here I stand, true to you unto death!

*Senta leaps into the sea; suddenly the sea heaves and whirlpools,*
*drowning The Flying Dutchman and its crew.*

*In the glow of the rising sun, the transfigured forms of the Holländer and Senta,*
*are seen embraced in each other's arms,*
*rising over the wreck of the ship in the sea, and soaring to the heavens.*

**END of OPERA**

2:17:05

## DICTIONARY OF OPERA AND MUSICAL TERMS

**Accelerando** - Play the music faster, but gradually.

**Adagio** - At a slow or gliding tempo, not as slow as largo, but not as fast as andante.

**Agitato** - Restless or agitated.

**Allegro** - At a brisk or lively tempo, faster than andante but not as fast as presto.

**Andante** - A moderately slow, easy-going tempo.

**Appoggiatura** - An extra or embellishing note preceding a main melodic note. Usually written as a note of smaller size, it shares the time value of the main note.

**Arabesque** - Flourishes or fancy patterns usually applying to vocal virtuosity.

**Aria** - A solo song usually structured in a formal pattern. Arias generally convey reflective and introspective thoughts rather than descriptive action.

**Arietta** - A shortened form of aria.

**Arioso** - A musical passage or composition having a mixture of free recitative and metrical song.

**Arpeggio** - Producing the tones of a chord in succession rather than simultaneously.

**Atonal** - Music that is not anchored in traditional musical tonality; it does not use the diatonic scale and has no keynote or tonal center.

**Ballad opera** - Eighteenth-century English opera consisting of spoken dialogue and music derived from popular ballad and folksong sources. The most famous is *The Beggar's Opera,* which is a satire of the Italian opera seria.

**Bar** - A vertical line across the stave that divides the music into measures.

**Baritone** - A male singing voice ranging between bass and tenor.

**Baroque** - A style of artistic expression prevalent in the 17th century that is marked by the use of complex forms, bold ornamentation, and florid decoration. The Baroque period extends from approximately 1600 to 1750 and includes the works of the original creators of modern opera, the Camerata, as well as the later works by Bach and Handel.

**Bass** - The lowest male voice, usually divided into categories such as:

> **Basso buffo** - A bass voice that specializes in comic roles: Dr. Bartolo in Rossini's *The Barber of Seville.*

> **Basso cantante** - A bass voice that demonstrates melodic singing quality: King Philip in Verdi's *Don Carlos.*

> **Basso profundo** - the deepest, most profound, or most dramatic of bass voices: Sarastro in Mozart's *The Magic Flute.*

**Bel canto** - Literally, "beautiful singing." It originated in Italian opera of the 17th and 18th centuries and stressed beautiful tones produced with ease, clarity, purity, and evenness, together with an agile vocal technique and virtuosity. Bel canto flourished in the first half of the 19th century in the works of Rossini, Bellini, and Donizetti.

**Cabaletta** - A lively, concluding portion of an aria or duet. The term is derived from the Italian word "cavallo," or horse: it metaphorically describes a horse galloping to the finish line.

**Cadenza** - A flourish or brilliant part of an aria (or concerto) commonly inserted just before a finale. It is usually performed without accompaniment.

**Camerata** - A gathering of Florentine writers and musicians between 1590 and 1600 who attempted to recreate what they believed was the ancient Greek theatrical synthesis of drama, music, and stage spectacle; their experimentation led to the creation of the early structural forms of modern opera.

**Cantabile** - An indication that the singer should sing sweetly.

**Cantata** - A choral piece generally containing Scriptural narrative texts: the *St. Matthew Passion* of Bach.

**Cantilena** - Literally, "little song." A lyrical melody meant to be played or sung "cantabile," or with sweetness and expression.

**Canzone** - A short, lyrical operatic song usually containing no narrative association with the drama but rather simply reflecting the character's state of mind: Cherubino's "Voi che sapete" in Mozart's *The Marriage of Figaro.*

**Castrato** - A young male singer who was surgically castrated to retain his treble voice.

**Cavatina** - A short aria popular in 18th and 19th century opera that usually heralded the entrance of a principal singer.

**Classical Period** - A period roughly between the Baroque and Romantic periods, the late 18th through the early 19th centuries. Stylistically, the music of the period stresses clarity, precision, and rigid structural forms.

**Coda** - A trailer added on by the composer after the music's natural conclusion. The coda serves as a formal closing to the piece.

**Coloratura** - Literally, "colored": it refers to a soprano singing in the bel canto tradition. It is a singing technique that requires great agility, virtuosity, embellishments and ornamentation: The Queen of the Night's aria, "Zum Leiden bin ich auserkoren," from Mozart's *The Magic Flute*.

**Commedia dell'arte** - A popular form of dramatic presentation originating in Renaissance Italy in which highly stylized characters were involved in comic plots involving mistaken identities and misunderstandings. Two of the standard characters were Harlequin and Colombine: The "play within a play" in Leoncavallo's *I Pagliacci*.

**Comprimario** - A singer who performs secondary character roles such as confidantes, servants, and messengers.

**Continuo, Basso continuo** - A bass part (as for a keyboard or stringed instrument) that was used especially in baroque ensemble music; it consists of an independent succession of bass notes that indicate the required chords and their appropriate harmonies. Also called *figured bass, thoroughbass*.

**Contralto** - The lowest female voice, derived from "contra" against, and "alto" voice; a voice between the tenor and mezzo-soprano.

**Countertenor** - A high male voice generally singing within the female high soprano ranges.

**Counterpoint** - The combination of two or more independent melodies into a single harmonic texture in which each retains its linear character. The most sophisticated form of counterpoint is the fugue form, in which from two to six melodies can be used; the voices are combined, each providing a variation on the basic theme but each retaining its relation to the whole.

**Crescendo** - A gradual increase in the volume of a musical passage.

**Da capo** - Literally, "from the top"; repeat. Early 17th-century da capo arias were in the form of A B A, with the second A section repeating the first, but with ornamentation.

**Deus ex machina** - Literally "god out of a machine." A dramatic technique in which a person or thing appears or is introduced suddenly and unexpectedly; it provides a contrived solution to an apparently insoluble dramatic difficulty.

**Diatonic** - A major or minor musical scale that comprises intervals of five whole steps and two half steps.

**Diminuendo** - Gradually becoming softer; the opposite of crescendo.

**Dissonance** - A mingling of discordant sounds that do not harmonize within the diatonic scale.

**Diva** - Literally, "goddess"; generally the term refers to a leading female opera star who either possesses, or pretends to possess, great rank.

**Dominant** - The fifth tone of the diatonic scale; in the key of C, the dominant is G.

**Dramatic soprano or tenor** - A voice that is powerful, possesses endurance, and is generally projected in a declamatory style.

**Dramma giocoso** - Literally, "amusing (or humorous) drama." An opera whose story combines both serious and comic elements: Mozart's *Don Giovanni*.

**Falsetto** - A lighter or "false" voice; an artificially-produced high singing voice that extends above the range of the full voice.

**Fioritura** - It., "flowering"; a flowering ornamentation or embellishment of the vocal line within an aria.

**Forte, fortissimo** - Forte (*f*) means loud; mezzo forte (*mf*) is fairly loud; fortissimo (*ff*) is even louder; additional *fff*'s indicate greater degrees of loudness.

**Glissando** - Literally, "gliding." A rapid sliding up or down the scale.

**Grand opera** - An opera in which there is no spoken dialogue and the entire text is set to music, frequently treating serious and tragic subjects. Grand opera flourished in France in the 19th century (Meyerbeer); the genre is epic in scale and combines spectacle, large choruses, scenery, and huge orchestras.

**Heldentenor** - A tenor with a powerful dramatic voice who possesses brilliant top notes and vocal stamina. Heldentenors are well suited to heroic (Wagnerian) roles: Lauritz Melchior in Wagner's *Tristan und Isolde.*

**Imbroglio** - Literally, "intrigue"; an operatic scene portraying chaos and confusion, with appropriate diverse melodies and rhythms.

**Largo or larghetto** - Largo indicates a very slow tempo, broad and with dignity. Larghetto is at a slightly faster tempo than largo.

**Legato** - Literally, "tied" or "bound"; successive tones that are connected smoothly. The opposite of legato is staccato (short and plucked tones.)

**Leitmotif** - Literally, "leading motive." A musical fragment characterizing a person, thing, feeling, or idea that provides associations when it recurs.

**Libretto** - Literally, "little book"; the text of an opera.

**Lied** - A German song; the plural is "lieder." Originally, a German art song of the late 18th century.

**Lyric** - A voice that is light and delicate.

**Maestro** - From the Italian "master"; a term of respect to conductors, composers, directors, and great musicians.

**Melodrama** - Words spoken over music. Melodrama appears in Beethoven's *Fidelio* and flourished during the late 19th century in the operas of Massenet (*Manon* and *Werther*).

**Mezza voce** - Literally, "medium voice"; singing with medium or half volume. It is sometimes intended as a vocal means to intensify emotion.

**Mezzo-soprano** - A woman's voice with a range between soprano and contralto.

**Obbligato** - An accompaniment to a solo or principal melody that is usually played by an important, single instrument.

**Octave** - A musical interval embracing eight diatonic degrees; from C to C is an octave.

**Opera** - Literally, "work"; a dramatic or comic play in which music is the primary vehicle that conveys its story.

**Opera buffa** - Italian comic opera that flourished during the bel canto era. Highlighting the opera buffa genre were buffo characters who were usually basses singing patter songs: Dr. Bartolo in Rossini's *The Barber of Seville*; Dr. Dulcamara in Donizetti's *The Elixir of Love.*

**Opéra comique** - A French opera characterized by spoken dialogue interspersed between the musical numbers, as opposed to grand opera in which there is no spoken dialogue. Opéra comique subjects can be either comic or tragic.

**Operetta, or light opera** - Operas that contain comic elements and generally a light romantic plot: Strauss's *Die Fledermaus*, Offenbach's *La Périchole*, and Lehar's *The Merry Widow.* In operettas, there is usually much spoken dialogue, dancing, practical jokes, and mistaken identities.

**Oratorio** - A lengthy choral work, usually of a religious nature and consisting chiefly of recitatives, arias, and choruses, but performed without action or scenery: Handel's *Messiah.*

**Ornamentation** - Extra embellishing notes—appoggiaturas, trills, roulades, or cadenzas—that enhance a melodic line.

**Overture** - The orchestral introduction to a musical dramatic work that sometimes incorporates musical themes within the work. Overtures are instrumental pieces that are generally performed independently of their respective operas in concert.

**Parlando** - Literally, "speaking"; the imitation of speech while singing, or singing that is almost speaking over the music. Parlando sections are usually short and have minimal orchestral accompaniment.

**Patter song** - A song with words that are rapidly and quickly delivered. Figaro's "Largo al factotum" in Rossini's *The Barber of Seville* is a patter song.

**Pentatonic** - A five-note scale. Pentatonic music is most prevalent in Far Eastern countries.

**Piano** - A performance indication for soft volume.

**Pitch** - The property of a musical tone that is determined by the frequency of the waves producing it.

**Pizzicato** - An indication that notes are to be played by plucking the strings instead of stroking the string with the bow.

**Polyphony** - Literally, "many voices." A style of musical composition in which two or more independent melodies are juxtaposed; counterpoint.

**Polytonal** - Several tonal schemes used simultaneously.

**Portamento** - A continuous gliding movement from one tone to another through all the intervening pitches.

**Prelude** - An orchestral introduction to an act or a whole opera that precedes the opening scene.

**Presto, prestissimo** - Vigorous, and with the utmost speed.

**Prima donna** - Literally, "first lady." The female star or principal singer in an opera cast or opera company.

**Prologue** - A piece sung before the curtain goes up on the opera proper: Tonio's Prologue in Leoncavallo's *I Pagliacci.*

**Quaver** - An eighth note.

**Range** - The span of tonal pitch of a particular voice: soprano, mezzo-soprano, contralto, tenor, baritone, and bass.

**Recitative** - A formal device used to advance the plot. It is usually sung in a rhythmically free vocal style that imitates the natural inflections of speech; it conveys the dialogue and narrative in operas and oratorios. *Secco*, or dry, recitative is accompanied by harpsichord and sometimes with other continuo instruments; *accompagnato* indicates that the recitative is accompanied by the orchestra.

**Ritornello** - A refrain, or short recurrent instrumental passage between elements of a vocal composition.

**Romanza** - A solo song that is usually sentimental; it is shorter and less complex than an aria and rarely deals with terror, rage, or anger.

**Romantic Period** - The Romantic period is usually considered to be between the early 19th and early 20th centuries. Romanticists found inspiration in nature and man. Von Weber's *Der Freischütz* and Beethoven's *Fidelio* (1805) are considered the first German Romantic operas; many of Verdi's operas as well as the early operas of Wagner are also considered Romantic operas.

**Roulade** - A florid, embellished melody sung to one syllable.

**Rubato** - An expressive technique, literally meaning "robbed"; it is a fluctuation of tempo within a musical phrase, often against a rhythmically steady accompaniment.

**Secco** - "Dry"; the type of accompaniment for recitative played by the harpsichord and sometimes continuo instruments.

**Semitone** - A half step, the smallest distance between two notes. In the key of C, the half steps are from E to F and from B to C.

**Serial music** - Music based on a series of tones in a chosen pattern without regard for traditional tonality.

**Sforzando** - Sudden loudness and force; it must stand out from the texture and be emphasized by an accent.

**Singspiel** - Literally, "song drama." Early German style of opera employing spoken dialogue between songs: Mozart's *The Magic Flute.*

**Soprano** - The highest range of the female voice ranging from lyric (light and graceful quality) to dramatic (fuller and heavier in tone).

**Sotto voce** - Literally, "below the voice"; sung softly between a whisper and a quiet conversational tone.

**Soubrette** - A soprano who sings supporting roles in comic opera: Adele in Strauss's *Die Fledermaus*; Despina in Mozart's *Così fan tutte.*

**Spinto** - From the Italian "spingere" (to push); a singer with lyric vocal qualities who "pushes" the voice to achieve heavier dramatic qualities.

**Sprechstimme** - Literally, "speaking voice." The singer half sings a note and half speaks; the declamation sounds like speaking but the duration of pitch makes it seem almost like singing.

**Staccato** - Short, clipped, detached, rapid articulation; the opposite of legato.

**Stretto** - Literally, "narrow." A concluding passage performed in a quick tempo to create a musical climax.

**Strophe** - Strophe is a rhythmic system of repeating lines. A musical setting of a strophic text is characterized by the repetition of the same music for all strophes.

**Syncopation** - A shifting of the beat forward or back from its usual place in the bar; a temporary displacement of the regular metrical accent in music caused typically by stressing the weak beat.

**Supernumerary** - A "super"; a performer with a non-singing and non-speaking role: "Spear-carrier."

**Symphonic poem** - A large orchestral work in one continuous movement, usually narrative or descriptive in character: Franz Liszt's *Les Preludes*; Richard Strauss's *Don Juan, Till Eulenspiegel,* and *Ein Heldenleben.*

**Tempo** - The speed at which music is performed.

**Tenor** - The highest natural male voice.

**Tessitura** - The usual range of a voice part.

**Tonality** - The organization of all the tones and harmonies of a piece of music in relation to a tonic (the first tone of its scale).

**Tone poem** - An orchestral piece with a program.

**Tonic** - The principal tone of the key in which a piece is written. C is the tonic of C major.

**Trill** - Two adjacent notes rapidly and repeatedly alternated.

**Tutti** - All together.

**Twelve-tone** - The twelve chromatic tones of the octave placed in a chosen fixed order and constituting, with some permitted permutations and derivations, the melodic and harmonic material of a serial musical piece. Each note of the chromatic scale is used as part of the melody before any other note is repeated.

**Verismo** - Literally "truth"; the artistic use of contemporary everyday material in preference to the heroic or legendary in opera. A movement particularly in Italian opera during the late 19th and early 20th centuries: Mascagni's *Cavalleria rusticana*.

**Vibrato** - A "vibration"; a slightly tremulous effect imparted to vocal or instrumental tone to enrich and intensify sound, and add warmth and expressiveness through slight and rapid variations in pitch.

*Opera Journeys™ Mini Guide Series*

*Opera Journeys™ Libretto Series*

*Opera Classics Library™ Series*

*A History of Opera: Milestones and Metamorphoses*

*Puccini Companion: the Glorious Dozen*

*Mozart's da Ponte Operas*

*Fifty Timeless Opera Classics*

## PUCCINI COMPANION: THE GLORIOUS DOZEN

**756-page Soft Cover volume**

### Each Puccini Chapter features:

**COMPLETE LIBRETTO**
Italian-English side-by-side

**STORY NARRATIVE**
with 100s of Music Highlight Examples

**ANALYSIS AND COMMENTARY**

### Print or Ebook

---

## A HISTORY of OPERA: MILESTONES and METAMORPHOSES

**432 pages, soft cover / 21 chapters**
*featuring*           **Over 250 music examples**
• A comprehensive survey of milestones in opera history
• All periods are analyzed in depth:
Baroque, Classical, Romantic, Bel Canto, Opera Buffa, German
Romanticism, Wagner and music drama, Verismo,
plus analyses of the "Tristan Chord," atonalism, minimalism...

### Print or Ebook

---

## OPERA JOURNEYS' COLLECTION: FIFTY TIMELESS OPERA CLASSICS

**816-page Soft Cover volume**

### Print or EBook

*A collection of fifty·of the most popular operas
in the Opera Journeys Mini Guide Series,
each with Story Narrative and 100s of Music Examples,
PLUS insightful,in delpth commentary and analysis*

---

## MOZART'S DA PONTE OPERAS:

### Don Giovanni, The Marriage of Figaro, Così fan tutte

**348-page Soft or Hard Cover Edition**

### Print or Ebook

**Mozart: Master of Musical Characterization;
Da Ponte: Ambassador of Italian Culture.**

*Featuring: Principal Characters, Brief Story Synopsis, Story Narrative,
Music Highlight Examples, and insightful in depth Commentary and
Analysis, PLUS a newly translated LIBRETTO of each opera
with Italian/English translation side-by-side.*

---

ORDER: Opera Journeys' Web Site www.operajourneys.com

# OPERA JOURNEYS LIBRETTO SERIES

### Print or Ebook

## *New translations (side-by-side) with Music Highlight Examples*

•Aida   •The Barber of Seville   •La Bohème
•Carmen   •Cavalleria Rusticana   •La Cenerentola
•Così fan tutte   •Don Carlo   •Don Giovanni
•La Fanciulla del West   •Gianni Schicchi
•Lucia di Lammermoor   •Madama Butterfly
•The Magic Flute   •Manon Lescaut
•The Marriage of Figaro   •A Masked Ball
•Otello   •I Pagliacci   •Rigoletto   •La Rondine
•Salome   Samson and Delilah   •Suor Angelica
•Il Tabarro •Tosca •La Traviata •Il Trovatore •Turandot

---

# OPERA JOURNEYS MINI GUIDE SERIES

### Print or Ebook

## *featuring 125 titles*

- *Brief Story Synopsis*

- *Principal Characters*

- *Story Narrative*

- *Music Highlight Examples*

- *Commentary and Analysis*

•The Abduction from the Seraglio •Adriana Lecouvreur •L'Africaine •Aida •Andrea Chénier
•Anna Bolena •Ariadne auf Naxos •Armida •Attila •The Ballad of Baby Doe •The Barber of Seville
•Duke Bluebeard's Castle •La Bohème •Boris Godunov •Candide •Capriccio •Carmen
•Cavalleria Rusticana •Cendrillon •La Cenerentola •La Clemenza di Tito •Le Comte Ory
•Così fan tutte •The Crucible •La Damnation de Faust •The Death of Klinghoffer •Doctor Atomic
•Don Carlo • Don Giovanni •Don Pasquale •La Donna del Lago •The Elixir of Love •Elektra
•Ernani •Eugene Onegin •Exploring Wagner's Ring •Falstaff •La Fanciulla del West •Faust
•La Fille du Régiment •Fidelio •Die Fledermaus •The Flying Dutchman •Die Frau ohne Schatten
•Der Freischütz •Gianni Schicchi •La Gioconda •Hamlet •Hansel and Gretel •Henry VIII
•Iolanta •L'Italiana in Algeri •Les Huguenots •Iphigénie en Tauride •Julius Caesar •Lakmé
•Lohengrin •Lucia di Lammermoor •Macbeth •Madama Butterfly •The Magic Flute
•The Makropolis Case •Manon •Manon Lescaut •Maria Stuarda •The Marriage of Figaro
•A Masked Ball •Die Meistersinger •The Mikado •Nabucco •Nixon in China •Norma
•Of Mice and Men •Orfeo ed Euridice •Otello •I Pagliacci •Parsifal •The Pearl Fishers
•Pelléas et Mélisande •Porgy and Bess •Prince Igor •I Puritani •The Queen of Spades
•The Rake's Progress •The Rape of Lucretia •The Rhinegold •Rigoletto •The Ring of the Nibelung
•Roberto Devereaux •Rodalinda •Roméo et Juliette •La Rondine •Der Rosenkavalier •Rusalka
•Salome •Samson and Delilah •Show Boat •Siegfried •Simon Boccanegra •La Sonnambula
•Suor Angelica •Susannah •Il Tabarro •The Tales of Hoffmann •Tannhäuser •Thaïs •Tosca
•La Traviata •Tristan and Isolde •Il Trittico •Les Troyens •Il Trovatore •Turandot
•Twilight of the Gods •The Valkyrie •Werther •West Side Story •Wozzeck

ORDER: Opera Journeys' Web Site www.operajourneys.com

Made in the USA
Middletown, DE
20 January 2020